The Art of Sensitive Parenting

The Art of Sensitive Parenting

The 10 Master Keys to Raising Confident, Competent, and Responsible Children

Katharine C. Kersey, Ed.D.

Illustrations by Rob Lauer

ACROPOLIS BOOKS LTD.
WASHINGTON, D.C.

Reprinted 1988

ACROPOLIS BOOKS, LTD.
Colortone Building, 2400 17th St., N.W.
Washington, D.C. 20009

Printed in the United States of America by
COLORTONE PRESS
Creative Graphics, Inc.
Washington, D.C. 20009

Attention: Schools and Corporations
ACROPOLIS books are available at quantity discounts with bulk purchase for educational, business, or sales promotional use. For information, please write to: SPECIAL SALES DEPARTMENT, ACROPOLIS BOOKS LTD., 2400 17th ST., N.W., WASHINGTON, D.C. 20009.

**Are there Acropolis Books you want
but cannot find in your local stores?**
You can get any Acropolis book title in print. Simply send title and retail price, plus 50 cents per copy to cover mailing and handling costs for each book desired. District of Columbia residents add applicable sales tax. Enclose check or money order only, no cash please, to: ACROPOLIS BOOKS LTD., 2400 17th ST., N.W., WASHINGTON, D.C. 20009.

Library of Congress Cataloging in Publication Data

Kersey, Katharine C.,
   Sensitive parenting.

   Includes index.
   1. Parenting—Handbooks, manuals, etc.
I. Title.
HQ755.85.K47   1983   649'.1   83-15600
ISBN 0-87491-700-X
ISBN 0-87491-713-1 (pbk.)

Acknowledgments

This book would not be a reality today if it were not for my student/teaching assistant/friend, Susan Vorhis, who said, "You should write a book. Let me help you." She convinced me that I had something worthwhile to say. She is the one who stayed behind me in my search for a publisher, who spent hours working with me during her spring break and then took another week to go with me to the beach to proofread, type and bounce ideas around.

Usually we think the teacher guides the student, and I hope I have had that place in her life—but I can honestly say that I owe her much—more than I can ever say for her confidence and hours of work which she gave to me to help make this dream a reality.

I want to express gratitude also:

To my children, Barbara Leigh, David and Marc, who are the sole reasons for my desire to figure out what "parenting" is all about. They have indeed been my teachers and I am still learning and growing—because of them.

To my husband, Wilbur, who has known me since I was seven, loved me since I was eleven and been married to me since I was twenty-one—who has been patient with all my changing needs and struggles—who has given me the space I needed to stretch and grow and who has continued to love and support me through it all.

To Fae, my friend for 23 years—whose children grew up with mine and provided for us many discussions which led to the convictions expressed in this book. I am grateful to her also for letting us hide away in her beach cottage for the last week of this book's birth.

To my students through the years who provided many of the observations recounted in this book and who have kept me mentally alert with their questions and concerns and stimulated and inspired me to keep searching for answers.

Contents

Preface

Children are given to us—on loan—for a very short period of time. They come to us like a packet of flower seeds, with no pictures on the cover, and no guarantees. We don't know what they will look like, be like, act like, or have the potential to become.

Our job, like the gardener's, is to meet their needs as best we can: to give proper nourishment, love, attention, and caring, and to hope for the best. The gardener learns to be "tuned in" to the plant. If it thrives in its environment, he leaves it alone. If, however, it is not growing as it should, or its leaves are withering, the gardener makes some changes. He watches for signs of lack of nourishment. He knows that all plants are different, need varying amounts of care and attention, and grow at different rates of speed.

He knows when and how to water each variety. When a leaf withers, he throws it away, but does not give up on the entire plant. He expects both brown leaves and healthy ones.

Children need to be treated in much the same way. Parents need to "tune in" to signs of healthy growth and development as well as signs of trouble. If a child needs a little extra attention and help (because of the birth of a new baby, a move, or starting in a new school), the parent should give it—knowing that in time, when the adjustment is made, the child will be back to normal. If, when a child makes mistakes and falls, we understand that it's a necessary part of growth, we can continue to believe in his potential and let him know that we have faith in his future.

As the gardener enjoys watching the growing plant develop its God-given natural beauty, so the parent marvels as the growing child evolves into a work of art—unique and different from any other living creature.

The gardener thrills at the beauty of the carnation as well as that of the rose. He sees their individual strengths rather than their weaknesses. The carnation may be sturdier and longer-lasting than the fragile rose, but each is beautiful in its unique fashion.

Every gardener knows that a rosebush won't produce carnations, but it's not easy for parents to tell whether their youngster is a "rose," or a "carnation." This child who realizes that he never quite measures up to the expectations of the parent can give up and stop trying.

Our goal for children is to help them become confident, competent, independent, fully functioning human beings. We have only a few years in which to accomplish this task. Effective parenting requires a delicate balance between setting limits as long as they are necessary and letting go as soon as possible. When our children are very young and completely dependent, we give them a trusting, safe environment where they feel wanted, loved, and important. Then, as they grow and can assume responsibility for themselves, we gradually encourage them to "do" for themselves. We help them learn how to make choices and live with the consequences of their actions, offering encouragement along the way. Gradually more and more decision-making is turned over to them—so that by the time they're sixteen, they know what's good for them: how much they need to rest, how much they need to eat, how much they need to study.

When children are free and encouraged to discover their own strengths, likes, abilities, aptitudes, and body rhythms, they come to know, appreciate, accept, and like themselves. A child who is a "carnation" does not waste his time and energy longing or trying to be a "rose."

And when children learn how to make their own good decisions, they grow up feeling good about themselves—with little need to "follow the crowd" or give in to peer pressure. When they leave home for the first time, they do not find it necessary to experiment, test the limits, defy authority, damage their bodies, sacrifice their goals, and risk their futures. When parents take too much responsibility for their children and hold on to their power too long, children remain dependent and irresponsible, and resent us for it. They then start to defy us, break our rules, and rebel against all authority.

Children do not need perfect parents, but they do need parents who assume responsibility for their own lives—who attempt to keep their own lives in order. It's important for our children to know that we are all separate individuals—with different needs, likes, personalities, strengths and weaknesses—who at times derive help and satisfaction from being together, and at times must manage alone.

Our children start out as totally dependent creatures. If we have done our job well, the day will come when they have outgrown their need for us, and are comfortable with their separateness. No longer will they be dependent upon us for financial, emotional, or physical support. Then, and only then, can we become lifetime friends who relate to each other as independent, healthy, mature adults—alike in some ways and different in others—who love and appreciate each other and, best of all, enjoy each other's company.

Introduction

I have spent my whole professional life—actually, ever since I became a parent 24 years ago—thinking about how we can motivate children in positive ways. We need methods that will not antagonize them or give them a need to rebel, disobey, or invalidate all that we stand for and want to pass on to them.

When I first tried to figure out how to be a parent, I was sure that everyone else knew more than I, so I watched what other mothers, fathers, teachers, and grandparents did when they were caring for children. It became apparent to me very early—when I watched a mother spank her child, for example—that instead of his promptly trying to obey her (as she had hoped) he reacted in other ways. I began to notice something that other people didn't seem to see: I watched what the child did *next*. I found that he sulked, withdrew, cried, flung back at her, pinched another child, bit his little brother, spilled the juice, tore a book, marked up the wall, or kicked the dog. It was obvious that his energy was focused not on trying to please his mother, but rather on managing the emotion that she had introduced into the scene—the embarrassment, hurt, or anger.

I soon became a "student" of children. It became my personal crusade to develop principles to learn and live by that would effectively and efficiently help our children grow in the direction best suited for them. I felt we needed principles that would lead them to become self-sufficient, content, competent, and socially adept. These principles should help them recognize the needs of others while understanding, speaking up, and looking out for themselves. Our goal is to raise children who can stand on their own two feet and relate to others in a healthful, mature, and caring way.

Through studying, teaching, living with, and working on behalf of children, I have developed ten principles, which I believe can guide us to more productive interactions and relationships with children. The case studies used to illustrate these principles are all actual events—observed first-hand by myself or my students. As I share this ten-step guide, or ten-week "crash course" in parenting with you, I hope you find it useful in discovering how to relate to children in a more sensitive, helpful, and positive way.

Chapter One

Treat the Child with Respect

The first principle—and this is crucial—is that we treat the child with respect. For some reason many of us seem to have inherited a disrespectful attitude toward children. We tend to talk down to them, embarrass them, command them, and order them around. As the years go by, if we repeatedly talk down to the child, we begin to build a wall that separates us. Eventually that wall gets so high that there's no scaling it. The child doesn't want us in his world anymore. He shuts us out. He lets others in but not us, because that wall is so high and is filled with so many hurts.

No one likes to be bossed around or embarrassed, and if we are, our normal response is negative. "Forget it! No way!" "I don't want to! You do it!" "You can't make me!" I think we pay a high price when we put a child down.

What we need to do instead is to respect him as a person. We need to help him feel that he is just as important as any other and deserves the same personal regard. (That doesn't mean he has as much power. But as a *person* he is as important.)

One little girl said to her mother, "Could we go out to lunch and pretend that I'm Kate—your best friend?" Her mother said, "Well, sure, we can go out to lunch, but why do you want to pretend that you're Kate?" "Because you and Kate always laugh and have fun together," was the child's sad response.

It is easy to forget that children have the same feelings and needs—including fear of ridicule and embarrassment—that adults have. If we can quickly get in the habit of putting ourselves in their place ("How would I feel if someone said that to me?") we can build bridges instead of barricades, and watch our relationships with our children grow both stronger and easier as the years pass.

Children Have the Same Feelings and Needs That We Have

Daddy had taken time off from work to come and see Sara compete in her first swim meet. She had been watching for her parents and was ecstatic when she saw them arrive. It was almost time for the meet to begin, and the "six and unders" were first.

The coach called for the swimmers to line up at the starting blocks. Daddy and Mother found chairs in the front row. Sara took her place, turning every few seconds to wave to her parents.

"Swimmers take your marks; go!" The gun sounded.

All of a sudden, Sara froze. She tried to dive in the pool, but for some reason her feet wouldn't move. She was scared to death.

"Go, Sara," the coach called. "Go!"

"Go on, Sara," her father encouraged from the sidelines.

Sara looked down and saw that the other children were already halfway across the pool. She knew it was too late—she had missed her chance.

The coach came up to her and said, "What happened? Why didn't you swim? You can do it. You've done it many times in practice. What happened?"

"I don't know," Sara hung her head. "I just got scared, I guess. I'm sorry." She started to cry.

Slowly she walked toward her parents.

"Don't come over here," Daddy said. "I don't want to see you. I took

time off work to see you swim, and you didn't even get wet. I don't want to have anything to do with you. I don't want to see your face. Go away. I don't even want to look at you." He turned his chair so that he couldn't see his daughter.

Sara was shocked. She sobbed harder. "But Daddy, I'm sorry. Please talk to me. Please," she begged.

"Get out of my sight. Go sit with the babies," Daddy insisted stubbornly.

The child became hysterical. She was uncontrollable. Mother handed Sara a towel and told her to wipe her eyes.

Daddy chided his wife, "Don't baby her, for goodness sake. She'll never grow up if you accept this infantile behavior. She belongs in the baby pool. I don't know why I wasted my day to see her act like a baby. C'mon, let's go. I have more important things to do."

Sara was devastated. After her parents left she found an out-of-the-way hiding place and threw herself face down on her towel, sobbing.

Even though Sara's father may have thought he could shame her into more acceptable behavior, the effect on her of his words and attitude could cause serious damage for a long time to come.

Children deserve to be treated with the same respect we give other people we love and care about. Many of us are more considerate of the feelings of strangers than we are of those of our own children.

Unfortunately we sometimes reflect the demeaning attitude toward children that our own parents may have displayed toward us. We feel that we have the right to humiliate and talk down to children when we wouldn't dream of talking that way to our friends. Perhaps we're afraid of losing our "power," or that our children won't take us seriously. Whatever the reason, each time we make them feel small, unimportant, dumb, or inadequate, we add to the wall between them and us. By treating our children with insensitivity, we give them a need to get back at us.

The child will win this battle in the end. He may wait until his adolescent years, but he will eventually find a way to even the score—with rebellion, lack of motivation, disrespect, delinquency, or disregard for the values with which he was raised.

Parents who learn early to be sensitive to the feelings of their children, and treat them the way they would like to be treated themselves, will find the dividends great. They will not suffer the humiliation and heartache in later years that often come to those who have habitually used disrespect as a fast and easy shortcut to compliance or obedience.

> Peter's father was graduating from law school, and all the relatives had come long distances for the celebration. Six-year-old Peter sat quietly and patiently through the hour-and-a-half ceremony. When it was over, the family gathered outside on the steps for pictures and congratulations. Little Peter became restless, started to run around, brushed up against one of the large columns in front of the concert hall, and fell down.
>
> Peter's mother spotted him and called across the porch, "You clumsy klutz! Look what you've done! You're filthy. I knew you couldn't stay clean for five minutes. Look at you. Your daddy will be ashamed of you." By this time she was at his side, hitting at his clothing,

presumably brushing off the dust. Her hitting, fussing, and name-calling caused others to look up and listen.

Peter was embarrassed. His eyes filled with tears and he hung his head. His mother took him by the hand and hurried him to the car. She told him to sit there and wait for them, since he didn't know how to stand still and not get dirty. She returned to the relatives and friends on the steps while Peter sat alone, waiting, in the car.

On special occasions, parents are frequently tired, excited, or nervous, especially with a houseful of out-of-town guests and a great deal of entertaining to do. Children invariably get the worst of the deal. They can usually sense that things are not quite normal, and frequently pick up their parents' anxiety. Most often they're not included in the adult conversation, and have no choice but to fend for themselves and seek their own diversion.

When parents embarrass children in public—in front of family members, friends, even strangers—it can be a devastating experience for the child. In

Peter's case, he will probably connect his father's graduation from law school with shame, embarrassment, and unpleasant memories.

No one would think of yelling at an adult for doing something careless or negligent in a similar social situation. In fact this very mother, not an hour later at a crowded reception, bumped into a china cabinet and knocked three shelves of dishes to the floor. Everyone was extremely generous, kind and forgiving, and the hostess insisted that the dishes could be replaced. No one thought of yelling at the mother, nor calling her a "clumsy klutz." If they had, she would have been devastated.

Children have the same feelings as adults. The difference is that they are usually helpless and have to take whatever is dished out to them. If they speak up for their rights, parents are likely to punish them more for their "lack of respect," or impudence.

Embarrassing your child is costly. It takes a toll on the child's self respect as well as on his feeling toward the adult in charge. If given this treatment as a steady diet, the child will show the effects sooner or later. He may become disrespectful, aggressive, sullen, apathetic, or insensitive—all distressing traits in children which we should do everything in our power to prevent.

> Mother was hurrying to get dinner ready for company before leaving for a meeting. Lori, age twelve, burst in and asked where her school pictures were. "I want to show them to Aunt Kim."
>
> "I don't know," Mother said. "I think they're in the hutch."
>
> Lori went into the dining room and began rummaging through a drawer.
>
> The telephone rang and Mother answered, then stretched the cord into the dining room to tell Lori the call was for her.
>
> When Mother saw the contents of the drawer spread on the table, she looked disgusted. "Lori, is that the hutch?" She pointed to the cupboard on the other side of the room. "It has been right there for five years! Get the cotton out of your head. When will you listen?"
>
> Handing Lori the phone, she said, "This is Marguerite. Tell her you can't hear because your ears are plugged up."
>
> Lori took the phone and escaped to the hall. Mother stashed the items in the drawer and returned to the kitchen.

Lori learned how little respect her mother had for her feelings when she embarrassed Lori both in front of her aunt and her friend on the telephone.

When Mother saw that Lori was looking in the wrong place, she could have calmly said, "The pictures are in the drawer of the hutch. That is the buffet, Lori."

Mother should have explained to Lori that she was in a hurry and would help her find the pictures after dinner was ready. If she had, Lori would probably have been more understanding. We often expect children to know what is on our minds without telling them.

Even when she became angry with Lori for dumping the contents of the drawer, she could have told her without being insulting. Whenever we belittle children in front of others it makes them resentful and hostile.

Certainly mother and daughter didn't feel very good about each other when they sat down to dinner.

Margaret was thrilled to be named to the safety patrol at school. She came bounding in the house to tell her mother the exciting news.

"Well, that's fine," said Mother, "but I want you to know that in order to stay on the patrol you are going to have to make all As and Bs. That shouldn't be hard because I know you're capable of doing that kind of work. I'm glad you have been made a patrol, and I hope that now you will be willing to work harder to keep your grades up."

Somewhat deflated, Margaret left the room muttering, "I don't see why I have to make good grades for you to let me be a patrol. After all, it was the teachers who picked me. They should be the ones to decide."

Calling after her, Mother said, "Well, they can make you a patrol, but I can decide whether or not you can remain one."

On her first report card, Margaret made all As and Bs. Mother told her she was proud of her. "I knew you could do it if you wanted to badly enough," she said.

On the next report card, Margaret made a C on social studies. The second six weeks had been particularly difficult because she had been sick for several days, and her father had been in the hospital. When she brought her report card home she kept it from her mother for twenty-four hours. When it was time to take it back to school, she brought it downstairs and left it on the kitchen table. When Mother saw the report card she was disappointed. She called Margaret and said, "You know what this means, don't you? You're going to have to give up being a patrol."

"But Mom, I couldn't help it," Margaret said. "I studied hard, but I missed some of the work this six weeks. I'll bring it up next six weeks, I promise. Give me one more chance. Please, Mom."

"I'm sorry, Margaret, I made a deal and the deal sticks. I'll write a note to your teacher tonight."

Margaret went to her room, threw her books on the floor, and turned on the radio. On the next report card there were three Cs.

Well-meaning parents often feel they can motivate their children by threatening to take away something special if the children do not meet certain standards. We pay a heavy price for snatching away something that children love. It has been my experience that when parents exercise this right, the side effects are not worth it.

If we as adults were to have something taken away from us—a privilege or hobby—because we displeased someone, we would feel resentful and hostile. For example, if our spouse, dissatisfied with the way we kept house, issued an ultimatum that we could not drive the car, go to any more movies, or visit our friends until we improved our housekeeping skills, I seriously doubt that this maneuver would work. Rather than trying to please him with better housekeeping techniques, many of us would retaliate by going where we wanted to or by generally defying him.

Children have the same feelings; they do not like to be threatened with ultimatums. Whenever we discuss expectations and consequences with them, we need to consider their feelings. Some deals we make are hard to live up to; we need to make sure our bargains are sensible and fair.

In the case mentioned above, I would respect the mother who admitted that her requirements had been too stringent. Since this had been a difficult six weeks for Margaret, her mother might agree to revise her original bargain. My hunch is that Margaret would work hard not to disappoint her mother, and to show her that her faith in her was well-founded.

Children Live Up to Their Labels

It was late in the school day, and everyone in the fourth grade was tired. The students were showing it by running around the class; the teacher was showing it by fussing at everyone in general and no one in particular.

Donald, sitting in the trash can and being extremely loud, was throwing trash on the floor and annoying the teacher. She finally said to him, "Don't you ever get tired of being a jerk?" Donald looked at her and laughed, until some of the other students began to call him a jerk. At that point he got angry and walked to his desk, kicking some of the children along the way. He retreated into a sullen mood and remained in it until his bus was called. As he was walking out the door, his teacher heard two of the children taunting him: "Donald is a jer-rk. Donald is a jer-rk."

This teacher expressed her frustrations by singling out one student. She called him a name and then left him to his own defenses to deal with the unhappy result. Her relationship with Donald was damaged and she modeled name-calling behavior, which the other students immediately picked up and imitated. All she had achieved was hurting one child's self esteem: the classroom was not quiet; order was not restored.

School days are long—for both students and teachers. It's easy for teachers to lose their cool by the end of the day. It might have helped if the teacher had admitted to the children and to herself that it had been a long day and that she felt tired and out of sorts and knew that they did too. She could have ignored Donald if he was not disturbing the others, while rewarding the students who

were behaving. (For example, she could announce that everyone who was sitting in his seat when she flicked the lights could subtract two examples from their math homework.)

She certainly had every right to deal openly with Donald's disruption, but she could have done so in a non-threatening way: "I know you must be restless. I feel the same way. Could you please find something else to do so that I won't get even more irritated with you?"

Teachers are human, too, of course, and do get tired and cross. But name-calling is counterproductive because labeling is disabling and invites resistance and resentment. Children derive their judgment of themselves from the judgment of others, and teachers are high on their list of importance. When teachers resort to harsh words, biting comments, and sarcastic tones, seeds of doubt are planted in the child's mind, and his self worth takes a tumble. He sees himself as a troublemaker, a nuisance, and a bother, and he is liable to devote even more energy into living up to the future that has been predicted for him.

Treat the
Child with
Respect

A class of first-grade students was taking a standardized test. Jane was having difficulty answering questions. The teacher noticed her and announced loud enough for the whole class to hear, "You still don't know how to do the problems, do you? I guess you'll be with us again next year."

Jane put her pencil down and stopped trying to complete the test. She gave up, after having her personal feeling of failure confirmed by the teacher in front of her classmates.

Instead of criticism, Jane needed encouragement to try to do her best on the test. The teacher could have helped by saying to her privately, "I'm proud of you for trying, even when the questions are hard. If there are problems you can't figure out, why don't you skip them and try others. You might find some that are easier for you."

Our goal as parents and teachers is to encourage children to keep on trying and to do their best. If we tell them they are going to fail, they probably will!

Mother and Father took Clayton, five, out to eat with his little sister. As soon as the family got to the restaurant, Mother began to lecture Clayton: "I don't know why I do this to myself. Every time we take you anywhere, you spoil it for us. You always act up and ruin things, and I know I'm going to wind up spanking you again, like I always do."

All through the cafeteria line, Mother kept adding sarcastic comments: "Don't even think about pushing your own tray, you'll only drop it. I'll order your meal, thank you. You always ask for the most expensive thing and then never eat it." Finally Clayton, who was slightly ahead of his mother, grabbed a handful of straws and made off with them, knocking over a basket of crackers in the process.

Furious, Mother chased Clayton through the cafeteria, and when she caught up with him, she whacked him on the seat of his pants. Throughout dinner, she continued to fuss. "Sit up straight. Don't mess with your food. Don't bother your sister or I'll bust you good."

The boy persisted in his irritating behavior, dropping food on the floor and slopping milk on his shirt. He asked to go to the bathroom and when his father got up to take him, Mother said, "He has the instincts of a puppy dog. He doesn't need to go—he just wants to make trouble."

Clayton wet his pants.

In this case, Mother was literally "asking for" what she got. All of her remarks to her son indicated that the kind of behavior she expected was less than perfect. She didn't give Clayton a chance to show what he was capable of, nor did she give him a chance to do anything for himself. He finally took some initiative by misbehaving. He lived right "down" to his mother's stated expectations.

In addition, Clayton probably felt that punishment was inevitable. His mother had as much as promised it—so he might as well "earn" it by doing something. Up until the time his mother spanked him, his behavior really had not been out of bounds. The spanking made him angry and desirous of revenge, which he achieved beautifully and in a way over which his mother had no control: he wet his pants!

Throughout the evening, Mother gave her son no indication of the standard of behavior she regarded as desirable. She only let him know what she anticipated, which he obediently delivered.

It would probably be wise for Mother to try the reverse tactic. She might talk with Clayton ahead of time about a reasonable standard to work toward. "If you wait quietly until our turn to be served, then you may help us select a table." "If we can get through the food line all together and peacefully, you may choose a dessert." At first, he might be given a tray to carry with only silverware, rolls, or something light or reasonably indestructible on it. Or he could be assigned responsibility for getting straws for everyone from the dispenser.

Parents can help to build responsible behavior in children by telling them what is expected and then rewarding them when they successfully complete small tasks leading to the goal. Children tend to live up to their labels, so we can help by being careful to make the labels we give them both positive and attainable.

Fill Your Child with Self-Esteem

> Mother and Father had taken their nine-year-old son out to dinner. When the son finished eating, he began to entertain himself by playing with a small plastic airplane. When he threw it in the air, it hit his father's glasses.
>
> His father flew into a rage. He became louder and louder as he said, "Don't you know how dangerous it is to throw things at people's faces? Suppose it had been a gun and you had aimed it at me. I have told you time and time again about this very thing!" Then Mother chimed in with, "Why do you always have to make trouble? You can never behave. You are always getting into mischief. We should have left you at home."
>
> Embarrassed, the boy cowered in his seat until his parents were ready to leave.

By embarrassing and insulting their son in public, these parents are only making matters worse. By labeling him a troublemaker and telling him that he never does anything right, they provide him with a negative image to live up to. Incidents such as this take a toll on the child's self-esteem; he begins to see himself as inadequate and unacceptable.

Children come into the world not knowing who they are. They learn who they are from those around them. They derive their "sense of self" from the attitudes reflected in the faces of those who are important to them—those who care for them, those who become the "significant others" in their lives.

Parents and caregivers are the child's first mirrors. When they respond with attention, cuddling, smiles, singing, and talking, he begins to believe that he is valuable. If, on the other hand, he is neglected, treated with indifference, fed absentmindedly (or with bottle propped), or ignored for long hours at a time, he develops a negative view of himself.

As children grow, they pick up vibrations from the other people around them: siblings, friends, relatives, babysitters, and eventually teachers. They try very hard to fit what they hear about themselves into a total picture. In other words, as Dorothy Briggs says in *Your Child's Self Esteem,* "Children value themselves to the degree that they have been valued. What they say about me is what I am!"

A child's behavior is a clue to his self-image. When children are sure of themselves, feel good about themselves, and like themselves, they are friendly, outgoing, and self confident. They have no need to misbehave, make trouble, annoy, and destroy. When children have a low opinion of themselves, they lack the courage and energy to tackle new problems. They are a problem to others; they hold back progress and are often doomed to misery and failure.

A good self-image is not to be confused with conceit. The latter is quite the opposite. In fact, conceit is merely whitewash used as an effort to cover up low self-esteem. A person with sincere self-respect is so secure that he does not need to impress others.

It is our job as parents, then, to raise emotionally healthy children who possess a solid sense of self-worth. We must enhance our children's self-esteem so that they will grow up to be constructive members of society who contribute to the peaceful ongoing of humankind, possess inner strength, and are able to enjoy successful involvement with others.

When children are confident, they become content, and the rewards for that contentment are far-reaching. Happy people know how to be successfully involved with others. They feel their lives are productive; they enjoy people and see the world as a good place.

Unhappy people make life miserable for others. They constantly find fault with those around them and the groups to which they belong. They are hostile destroyers and impediments to progress.

The key to happy living and inner peace is high self-esteem. It is perhaps the best gift we can give to a child.

Self-esteem builds the same way muscles do—with constant work and practice. Just as muscles provide strength for the body, self-confidence brings "inner sureness" and is the backbone of happiness and the foundation of a productive life.

Kathy, age sixteen, was ready to leave for school and came into the kitchen to tell Mother goodbye. Mother looked at her and said, "Are you going to school like that? Your hair looks horrible!"

Kathy was hurt and angered by her mother's words. She had also been made to feel self-conscious. She responded with, "What's wrong with my hair? I like it. It's not your hair. I don't tell you how to look."

Time ran out, and Kathy left for school—upset and feeling insecure about her hair.

Right before someone leaves the house is not the time to challenge the way she has chosen to dress. I question anyway whether we should inflict our opinions on teenagers concerning their choices of clothes and hair styles. By the time a child is sixteen, I think she should be allowed to dress as she chooses. If you have strong opinions, talk with her when time is not running out, and then only make suggestions.

Children usually come around to accept our values—eventually. But we need to be patient while they examine other lifestyles and preferences in an effort to establish their own identity.

Questions and Answers

Q. *Will you please discuss the widespread habit of several of my young married friends who toss their very young children (usually infants) into the air, or tickle them excessively? When I object (I have raised four), they laugh at me and say the babies love it. I cannot believe pediatricians consider this a harmless practice. The babies and young children do not look happy to me when being treated like this.*

A. I checked with a pediatrician who agreed with me that this could indeed be damaging and frightening to the child. Gentle fondling, tickling, and lifting can, of course, be pleasurable and should elicit a "delight response" with accompanying smiles and laughter from the infant. The quantity and quality of the behavior, however, is the important issue. Being tossed high into the air and being tickled excessively could make the child feel very insecure and could lead to hysteria in an older child. It could also cause tearing and bleeding of the periosteum (the connective tissue which protects the bones). In fact, if carried to an extreme, it might even suggest possible sadistic tendencies in the adult.

It is important to remember that young infants are excellent "sense detectors" and can pick up quickly on the vibrations and attitudes of those who handle and care for them.

Q. *My husband is constantly "on" our son every night at the dinner table, with "Sit up straight. Use your fork. Eat your peas. Don't talk with your mouth full. Use your napkin. Stop tipping the chair. Hurry up. Eat your dinner. Stop messing up your food. Where are your manners?"*

It honestly ruins dinner for me. I can see that this harassing makes our son worse. I have asked him to stop but it does no good. I start dreading dinner an hour ahead of time. I hate it, but feel powerless to stop it. Any suggestions?

A. Dinner time should be pleasant for everyone. I would talk very honestly with your husband and try to convince him of your seriousness. Tell him that you feel responsible for trying to make life more pleasant for all of you—especially during the little time that you are together. Ask him to please try it your way—no criticism—only kind remarks—for one week. Ask him if he will try it for your sake—and in return, you will do something special for him—bake a batch of his favorite cookies, for example. Appeal to his better nature. If he will try the new approach for one week, he will probably admit that dinner time is more pleasant. If one week is not enough, try another bargain for the next week.

Many adults feel that it is their responsibility to berate, correct, and criticize children in order to "shape them up." They need someone to point out to them that this approach is counter-productive—it in fact gives the children the necessary incentive to "keep up" the annoying behavior, rather than to put forth the effort required to eliminate it.

Q. *Our six-year-old daughter has announced that she is not going back to school. She says that her teacher yells and scares her to death. She says that she will go back to kindergarten or to another school, but she is not going back to this class. We tried your suggestions to the mother whose three-year-old didn't want to attend nursery school: we offered her rewards for going, arranged for a neighbor to take her, and tried to remain very firm. I've never seen her so determined. Do you have any suggestions?*

A. There must be a reason for her strong dislike of school. Since she says her teacher yells, perhaps it would be wise to begin with a conference with the teacher. You might tell her that your daughter seems to be afraid and ask her if she has any idea what is causing it. Then, if this does not solve the problem, you might talk with the principal. Suggest that perhaps there is a personality conflict between the child and her teacher and ask if he could move her to another class. Frequently when the school is made aware of problems uncovered by parents, they are more than willing to cooperate and attempt to find solutions.

Children who are shy or not accustomed to loud adults can become quite frightened when they are confronted with one. Sometimes their fear can immobolize them to such an extent that they are unable to concentrate or find joy in the discovery of learning.

Q. *My son, age seven, constantly threatens to run away from home. Usually I tell him to go ahead and even offer to help him pack his suitcase. Once I packed him a lunch and gave him a quarter for spending money. I actually feel sorry for him though, when he has to face defeat and return home. Is there a better way to handle this?*

A. I feel that a child who threatens to run away is really crying, "How important am I?" I think he needs assurance and the best response would be something that reassures him. ("Please don't run away. I would miss you too much.") If he does go anyway, when he comes back, try meeting him at the door with "I'm so glad you're home, I worried about you and missed you so much," rather than "What happened, did you get scared?"

Children are well aware of their own helplessness and when we rub it in ("What are you going to do when it gets dark?"), we only make them feel smaller and more dependent.

I feel we remain closer to our children when we listen carefully for the clues they give us and tell them what they need to hear.

Q. *My fifteen-year-old seems so moody and distant. Her attitude toward the whole family seems to be one of dislike and bare tolerance. She used to be pleasant and helpful. It seems as if her whole personality has changed, and we all find it hard even to like her. I feel myself flying off the handle and being sarcastic to her. This does no good, but her attitude is hard to accept. Is this natural? Will it end?*

A. Teenagers have much on their minds and they need a place where they don't have to work so hard to be accepted. They need some privacy, space, and time to sort out their feelings. Although I don't think we should allow them to be disrespectful, I do think we should try to make allowances for mood swings, silences, and grumpiness. Since they do not like themselves very much at this point in their life, it is natural that at times they exhibit traits that are difficult for us to like. Don't hesitate to tell her how you feel, but try not to shame or degrade her. Remember that this is a difficult time for her, and as she gains confidence and perspective, it, too, shall pass.

Q. *I am a junior in high school and my problem is my mother. She is constantly cutting me down—like you wouldn't believe. She even does it in* *front of my friends. She complains about everything I do. She makes fun of my hair, my clothes, my makeup, and my friends. She could win an award for being the most sarcastic mother of the year. I am even getting embarrassed for my friends to be around her.*

She is always telling me how grateful I should be and how much better I have it than she did. I'm sure this is true, but how can I help that? We can't even carry on a decent conversation anymore. She cuts my dad down too, but I guess he is used to it. Is there anything I can do to make her stop?

A. When parents get frustrated, they often take it out on their children. As teenagers grow and become more independent, mothers have to assume a different role and it is hard for many of them to shift gears.

I would suggest that you tell your mother you want to have a talk with her sometime when she feels like it. Then tell her that you wish you felt closer to her. Explain to her calmly that you feel you are growing apart and this makes you sad. Tell her that when she cuts you down or makes fun of you, you feel embarrassed and hurt.

If you are careful to maintain respect for her as you talk, I think your chances for her cooperation will be greater. I personally feel that she is lucky to have you concerned about the relationship. You'd better tell her before it gets to the point where you no longer care.

Suggestions for the Week

See how many of these you can check off this week.

1. Hold your child often.

2. Take time every day to really listen to what he has to say.

3. Let him cry, be hurt and angry.

4. Tell him that you love him often.

5. Spend time with him alone every day.

6. Look for something in him to praise every day.

7. Provide full-length mirrors and small hand mirrors in conspicuous places where he can see himself and watch his image change as he does.

8. Discuss his babyhood with him. Tell him of the cute things he did and how much you enjoyed him (and still do). Talk with him about who named him, how big he was, what his first words were and when he started walking.

9. Take a picture of your child doing different things and make a scrapbook which you can enjoy together. Keep adding to it.

10. Plan parties and special occasions for no reason—just because you are happy being together. Keep the party simple so he will enjoy it. It is a good rule of thumb for birthdays to invite as many people as his years of age.

11. Make him feel needed. Give him jobs to do that are his alone—which no one else will do if he forgets.

For older children:

1. Give them a private place of their own—a room, if possible, or at least a portion of a room—where they can keep private possessions and where no one will pry, clean up, or snoop.

2. Give each child a bulletin board—hung in a conspicuous place—where he can put pictures, papers, articles, collages, and drawings. Leave it to him to decorate and change the board as he wants.

Treat the
Child with
Respect

3. Take movies or make tapes of special occasions to save and play later for friends and relatives, and someday, grandchildren.

4. Take an interest in your children's friends. Learn their names. Invite them to the house and offer to cook pizza.

5. Help your children set goals for themselves and reach them. "What would you like to be able to do that you have not yet mastered? What can we do to help you meet these goals?"

6. Don't make them feel guilty when they want to cut the apron strings. Let them grow up. Be careful not to treat them the same way you did two years ago.

7. Encourage them to stretch in many directions. Introduce them to new experiences: watching people build, dance, teach, type, bake bread, decorate cakes, sail boats, whittle, refinish furniture, repair watches, install appliances, or wash cars.

8. Remember: the more capable children feel, the more skills they can master, the more obstacles they can hurdle—the more competent they will feel. Nothing builds success like success itself, and no one can succeed without first making mistakes.

Chapter Two

Make Sure That Privileges Are Earned

Parents need to be tireless disciplinarians. Without discipline, a child will be insecure, demanding, selfish, and self-centered. Because discipline means to teach and to train, it becomes the parent's job to teach and train the child. This takes patience, skill, confidence, and determination. It requires the ability to set limits, say "no," and be willing to be unpopular with your child.

One of the most important principles in effective discipline is to teach children that privileges and freedom go hand in hand with responsibility. It is crucial that children learn early that life is not a "free lunch." They won't get hand-outs, privileges, and freedom for nothing. There is a price.

We want our children to be motivated to work hard for what they want in life, to be able to set realistic goals and meet them and to be able to delay gratification and wait for the payoff.

Many children coming out of college today expect to start at the level of their parents. They are insulted to think that they need to start at the bottom and work up. Some are even willing to mooch off of their parents rather than live on a level to which they are unaccustomed or be bothered with jobs that are "beneath" them. They become bitter and dissatisfied when things don't work out to suit them.

Many of these children were given whatever they wanted—whenever they wanted it—without having to work, plan, or save for it. They grew up with the sad misconception that rewards in life come easily. They never really learned the satisfaction that comes from setting short- and long-term goals and then reaching them through effort and hard work.

When You Have... Then You May

A child can start becoming responsible early when his parent gently teaches him the concept of "When you have... then you may." We can start as soon as the child can walk. For example, when he takes off his pajamas, he can learn to put them where they belong instead of dropping them on the floor. "When you have put your clothes in the hamper, then I'll read you a story."

Then this concept can carry over into all areas of the child's life: "When you have swept the garage, then you may turn on the television." "When you've carried your dishes to the sink, then you may go to the playroom." "When you have made your bed, then you may go out to play."

After hearing this concept taught in class, one of my students said to her four-year-old, "When your pajamas are on, then I'll read you a story." And he said, "Huh?" She repeated her statement and he said, "I'm not going to put my pajamas on! I'm not your maid!" (His remark was priceless. Obviously he had been told that himself many times.) The mother had to bite her tongue to keep from saying anything, and she went into her bedroom and shut the door. From there she wrote down what he said to her, calling in monologue from the other room, "I'm not going to undress, I'm not your maid. I'm going to stay here all day..." "Well, I'll take my shirt off, but I'm not going to take my pants off..." "Well, I'll take my pants off, but I'm going to stay like this." (long silence)

"Well, I have my pajama bottoms on, but I'm not going to put the top on…"
And then there was a knock on her door, and with the books under his arm,
completely dressed, he said softly, "I'm ready for you to read to me now."

> Ben was paid $3.00 every week by his mother to cut the grass. One
> week he needed some extra money to go to the movies, so he asked
> her to advance him his pay. Reluctantly, Mother loaned him the $3.00.
>
> The next week Ben put off mowing the yard. Each time Mother
> reminded him, he gave her some excuse—it was too late, or wet, or he
> had a previous commitment. He became increasingly irritable and
> finally said, "Okay, okay! Get off my back. I'll do it!"
>
> When Saturday came, Ben still had not cut the grass. Mother, tired of
> hassling him, went out and mowed the lawn herself.
>
> Mother felt resentful toward her son and defeated because he had not
> lived up to his commitment. His feeling was that after the lapse in time
> and the extenuating circumstances, the subject should be dropped.

This is one of the saddest traps that parents fall into. Although most of us know that we need to teach our children to become responsible, it is difficult for us to watch them suffer and do without. It takes a great deal of strength and perseverance not to let them off the hook.

One of the biggest mistakes today's parents make is giving in to their children's demands and not requiring enough of them in return. Parents need to require more accountability from their children. For example, I don't recommend paying children allowances for chores done, because I think that members of the family ought to be willing to work for the good of all without financial remuneration. (I do think allowances are a good idea, however, when they are based on need. The child can learn the value of money from having to budget the way it is spent.)

When children have special needs and wants (a new flashlight, wallet, belt, or brand-name tennis shoes), that is a good time to encourage them to do "extra" jobs for pay around the house and the neighborhood. You might make deals with them: not for jobs that they should be doing already, but for extra jobs that need to be done or even habits you feel they need to acquire. For instance, "When you have cleaned out the hall closet, I will buy you the new flashlight," or "When you have gotten up the first time you are called, for 15 days, I will buy you the belt you have been wanting."

This approach serves several purposes: it makes the child more selective and cautious about things he asks for, and it helps him develop the ability to delay rewards and earn them, while at the same time improving his behavior and personal habits. He will be learning important skills that in the long run will make him happier with himself and easier for other people to love.

Children are better off not having everything they want. They will grow up to be less selfish and greedy and more appreciative, careful, and industrious, if we teach them early to plan and work for the goals that are important to them.

> Ernestine had been out of high school for two years—working, living at home, paying room and board, and making car payments. She had little left over to save.
>
> Her brother, Frankie, was a junior in high school. He was dying to have a car. According to him, all of his friends had cars and he was embarrassed to be dropped off at school in the mornings by Ernestine on her way to work.
>
> He kept pestering his parents to let him have a car. Although he had delivered papers some years ago and had bagged groceries at a super-market, school sports took all his time now, and he therefore had no source of income.
>
> One day he came home excited about a car a friend had seen on a used car lot.
>
> "Please, Mom, let's go look at it. Just look at it. That won't hurt anybody. I'm not asking you to get it—just take me to look at it," he said. "Johnny says it's got a great paint job, and the price is good. C'mon, please!"
>
> "But Frankie, you know how your father and I feel about a car," Mother said. "You don't have any money to buy one, and until you do, you'll just have to get rides with one of us. You know we'll always get you to school and pick you up on time."
>
> "But it's embarrassing. None of the other guys have to ride to school with a sister. C'mon, just look at it."
>
> "Okay, but just to look." Mother reluctantly gave in.
>
> When they got to the lot, Frankie spotted the car right away.

"Look, Mom. Hey, it's neat. Let's go for a test drive."

Overhearing their conversation, a salesman said, "Sure, help yourself. Drive your mom around the block. Take your time. This car's a real steal. Just came in today. I'm sure it won't be here long. Several other people have been in to look at it. It's the best buy on the lot. Here, just try it out."

Not wanting to disappoint Frankie, Mother gave in and they took the car for a test drive. As she watched his face, she knew she had made a mistake. She would never get out of this. The more enthusiastic he became, the more discouraged she was.

"Man, can you believe this? It drives without a sound—really smooth. Good gas mileage, too, I hear. I gotta have this car. Just lend me the money, Mom. I'll get a job. Johnny told me today about a job delivering prescriptions for the pharmacy—he says I can have it if I want. I'll be able to start making payments by the end of the month. C'mon Mom, please."

"But Frankie. You know that Ernestine had to save for a downpayment before we were willing to sign for her loan to get a car," Mother said. "It wouldn't be fair for us to let you have one when you don't have money to put down on it. And how would you pay for gas?"

"But she's a girl. Girls don't mind riding with other people. Besides she drives a lot farther every day than I would have to. I wouldn't need as much gas. I'd only go to school and back, I promise! All my friends have cars, Mom. I'm the only one who doesn't. I'm embarrassed to have to hitch rides with other guys. It seems like you and Dad would be embarrassed too. We're not poor, you know."

"Well, I don't know. I'll have to talk it over with your father."

Waiting for them, the salesman started in right away. "Just $500 down, and it's yours. How about it, son? Didn't I tell you you were going to love it? Like I said, it's the best buy on the lot. It won't be here by the weekend."

"Mom, what if somebody else gets it?" Frankie said. "Come on, I'll make *all* the payments—and I'll pay you back for the downpayment. Come On!"

"Well, I know boys are different. I guess I didn't understand how embarrassing it would be not to have your own car. Are you sure that you can get that job? We are certainly not going to make the payments, I can promise you that."

"Oh, yeah, I promise."

Mother reluctantly signed the papers, and Frankie drove the car home. Six months later, he had made one payment. His parents had made all the rest.

We do children no favors when we give them privileges without responsibility. In this case, Frankie had not demonstrated his ability to save money or delay gratification. By giving in to him, Mother was helping him remain irresponsible, impulsive, and demanding.

Children who are not taught to earn their privileges have a hard time accepting limitations. They are miserable when things don't go their way and make life miserable for those around them. They expect handouts all through life. Parents resent the burdens these children place on them, for they are usually ungrateful, demanding, and insensitive.

Although it is often hard for the soft-hearted, conscientious parent, one of the charges of good parenting is to help the child become self-reliant and able to assume responsibility. The child who is not forced to do this when he is young will have a harder time developing these skills as an adult.

If You Abuse It, You Lose It

The family had planned to go to the swimming pool together in the late afternoon, but in the meantime David wanted to go out and shoot baskets with his friends. Mother told him to be home at 4:00 so they could leave for the pool. When it was time to go swimming, David was not home. They waited about 15 minutes and still no David. Finally they rounded up his bathing suit and towel, got in the car and drove around looking for him. They tried a few of the neighbors' houses, using up more time, and finally found him nonchalantly shooting baskets in the driveway of a friend.

By the time David got in the car they were all exasperated with him, and his parents took turns fussing all the way to the pool. They told him how much of their time he had wasted, how inconsiderate and thoughtless he was, and how tired they were of his irresponsible behavior. By the time they arrived at the pool, they were worn out from their lecture, his sister was tired of listening to it, and David had not heard a word they said. They were all relieved to be at their destination.

David had been given no reason to obey his mother. He knew that he would still get to go to the pool, even if he was not home by 4:00. He had learned through past experience that he did not have to do what she said. Since his parents' lectures were repetitious and meaningless, he had learned to "tune them out."

In effect, David was rewarded for his misbehavior. Instead of having to be careful about the time, his parents took care of finding him and taking him to the pool. In fact, rather than having to walk home, he even received curb service!

When David wasn't home on time, I think his parents should have made sure that he missed out on going swimming. They might have left a note saying when they would return, or, if he could not have been left alone, one of them could have stayed back and let the others go. (Although this way the parent also suffers, the lesson taught is well worth it.) David would have learned that if he fails to obey the rules, he must suffer the consequences.

In other words, "if you abuse it, you lose it." If you don't obey the rules, you lose out on the privilege. That's the flip side of the "when... then" coin. It should be stated very simply, without scorn, ridicule or shaming: "Sorry, you abused it, you lose it." For example, if the child doesn't put his clothes in the hamper, "Sorry, no story." "What do you mean, no story?" "You didn't put your clothes in the hamper." "Oh, I forgot!" "You go and put your clothes in the hamper, and then I'll read you a story."

If a child goes out to play and hasn't made his bed, you don't need to lecture or scold him. You simply go out and call him, "Come on in." "Why?" "You didn't make your bed." He may have to *stay* in: "When you abuse it, you lose it—for today. But tomorrow I'm sure you'll remember."

I have a student who teaches two-year-old Downs' Syndrome children and she's developed a shrug of her shoulders that means, "You lost it." And when she does this to one of her little two-year-olds, they know to take a chair and pull it over to the wall. They look at her and sob softly. Then, in a few minutes, she indicates with another gesture, "Okay," and they come back. They knew what they did wrong without having to be told. They knew that they abused the privilege of playing with the other children.

When a child comes into a room and knocks everything down, or fights with somebody, or kicks or bites, or pulls somebody's hair, he loses it. "You lost your playtime. Sorry." Then he is moved someplace by himself. "But I bet tomorrow you'll remember." And if tomorrow he doesn't remember, then repeat the process.

A child who runs in the street loses the privilege of staying in the yard by himself—maybe for a week or a month—until you think he is able to control himself. Some children can play in the yard unsupervised when they're three, some when they're four, and others not until they're six. We find out what the child is capable of and we let him have that much freedom.

> Scott loved to play at Russell's home. This afternoon Mother said he could go provided he would be home by dark. Several times in the past, Scott had failed to return at the agreed-upon time.
>
> When it started getting dark and Scott had not returned, Mother became upset. She sent Brian, her younger son, to Russell's house to get Scott. Brian was captivated by the fun Scott and Russell were having and decided to join them.
>
> When it was dark, neither child was home, and Mother was angry. She went to get the boys. Lecturing all the way home, she berated Scott for acting so irresponsibly and for corrupting his younger brother. She punished Scott by taking away his TV privileges for a week and gave him the choice of a spanking or going to his room for the rest of the night.
>
> As it turned out, Mother gave Scott a double dose of punishment. Even though Brian also failed to do as he was told, he escaped her wrath and suffered no consequences. It is very likely that Scott resented his punishment and felt that he had been treated unfairly, since he was not the only one who disobeyed Mother.

It would have been better if the consequences had been discussed before Scott went to play with Russell (since this had been a recurring problem). He would have clearly understood that if he was not home on time, he would not be allowed to go to Russell's again for a week (or some other specified length of time). Then, if Scott was not home at dark, Mother could have called him, saying simply, "It is time to come home."

When he arrived, Mother could have told Scott that since he is not ready to handle playing away from home and coming back on time, he can play only in his own yard and must be in the house before dark. Since he abused the privilege of going to his friend's house, he has lost that privilege. Once he stays in for awhile, he may be given the chance to try again.

State Expectations in Advance

While his father was waiting for a prescription to be filled, Robbie romped up and down the aisles in the drug store. Seeing a table covered with lunch boxes, he picked one up and ran over to Daddy yelling, "I want this."

"No, go put it back," his father responded.

"I want it! I want it!"

"Put it back!"

Robbie threw the lunchbox on the floor, stomped his feet and said through clenched teeth, "I want that Dukes of Hazzard lunchbox!"

Daddy picked up the lunchbox and put in back on the table. He went to Robbie and said, "I'm not going to bring you out anymore. I should've left you home with your mother!"

At this, Robbie started screaming, and Daddy picked him up and swatted him on the backside.

By this time, the prescription was ready. Daddy paid for it, still holding the crying child. As they were leaving the store, Robbie saw the candy rack and pointed to it, sniffling, "I want some candy, Daddy."

"All right, pick out what you want." He put Robbie down so that he could make his selection.

From this experience, Robbie learned that when he throws a temper tantrum, his father will pay attention to him.

It would have been helpful if Daddy had stated his expectations before they left home. "Robbie, I want you to stay by my side at the drug store and not pick up anything. If you can remember, I will let you select a treat on the way out of the store."

Or, "If you will behave nicely while we are in the store, we can stop at the park on the way home and you can run and scream as much as you want. A store is not a place where you should run and stomp your feet."

Once a child has misbehaved or thrown a tantrum, a parent cannot afford to give him a treat. This will be reinforcement for his inappropriate actions, and the chances are great that he will repeat them to get another reward in the future.

Ed and Jim had overnight guests on Friday, and when their friends left the next morning, the boys' rooms were complete disasters.

Mother asked the boys to clean up their rooms, but they begged off, insisting that they wanted to watch their favorite television program. They promised to do their room later. An hour later, she asked again, but they found another excuse. An hour later, the same. Finally, in desperation, Mother went upstairs and cleaned the rooms herself.

When she finished, she angrily announced that they could not go out anywhere for the rest of the day, because they did not do as they were told.

The boys sulked and were miserable. They griped and complained about how unfair their punishment was. Mother continued to clean up and work around the house while they watched TV.

Nothing was accomplished by Mother's method of handling this situation. Mother played the martyr role and the boys assumed no responsibility for their actions.

These boys will continue to let their mother do the work unless she changes her tactics. It is a sad state of affairs when children are allowed to lie around watching TV while their parents do all the work. This does not teach them to be responsible, sensitive, or caring.

Children should help out at home—without having to be reminded. Living together as a family brings many privileges, but also means responsibilities.

Mother should have told the boys that she expected them to clean their rooms. It would have been wise for her to tell them *before* their friends arrived that they would be expected to clean up any mess that was made. (They might have been more cautious then—or even reminded their friends to put things away when they were finished with them.) She should have made it clear that they were not free to go out until the rooms were clean.

Then she should stick by her words. It is easier to be tough when you remember that you are helping your child to become a more responsible, confident, and competent person, and that you are also helping him become the kind of individual you find it easy to like. Loving our children is natural and easy. Liking them is sometimes another story.

Children at this age have a lot of energy which needs to be channeled into constructive and productive channels. They need to be industrious, considerate, and helpful. If these traits are not cultivated while they are young, when they grow up they will be happy to sit back and let others do the work. This attitude is certainly not a good one to carry into adulthood, marriage, or the working world.

> Chip and Elizabeth had come to spend six weeks with their father and stepmother, Emily. Since it was a beautiful day, Emily promised the children at breakfast that they could go to the pool for the afternoon. She rushed around all morning, trying to get her chores done and take care of the baby, so she would be able to go.

> At lunch, Emily told Chip and Elizabeth, "Hey, you guys, I've been working hard all morning, and so far you have done nothing but watch TV. Now, we have to get one thing straight. I'm not running a maid and taxi service here."

> After lunch, however, Chip and Elizabeth drifted back to the TV, while Emily cleaned up the dishes, fed the baby, and began to pack the car. The baby fussed as Emily went in and out of the house with playpen, diaper bag, bathing suits, and drinks.

> Finally, she had had it. "Okay, you guys. That's it. We're not going to the pool—in fact, not for the rest of the summer. I told you that I refused to be the cook, maid, and chauffeur for the next six weeks."

> Emily took the baby upstairs and left her stepchildren fussing in the den.

> As an outcome, Emily felt cheated: she had worked hard for the privilege of going to the pool and then she blew it by issuing the ultimatum to the children. They were mad, too. No one really got what he wanted.

The time to talk about expectations for the day is the first thing in the morning—or even the night before.

Emily needed to be up-front about the requirements for going to the pool: "I would like to take you to the pool this afternoon, but I need help from you. This is what I need: someone to make the beds, wash the breakfast dishes, fix the lunch, and entertain the baby. If each of you would select two jobs, I can do the rest. If all the jobs are done by 1:00, then we can leave for the pool."

This way, the children know ahead of time what is expected of them and what the pay-off will be. Emily would not feel like a martyr and the children would learn the important lesson of responsibility. Their next six weeks would be much improved if they start things off with mutual respect and understanding.

Aunt Julie needed to go to the grocery store to pick up a few items, and had taken Beth, four, with her. Once inside the store Beth decided that she wanted to ride in the basket section of the cart, and climbed in.

Aunt Julie pushed the cart near the food shelves, where items were within Beth's reach. When they came to the cookie section, Beth said, "Get me animal crackers, Aunt Julie." Her aunt agreed to the request and told her to grab a box.

When they got to the cereal shelves, Beth asked for something else. "Aunt Julie, can I have Captain Crunch?"

"No, you won't be at my house long enough to eat the whole box."

"But can I get them for Nanna's house? I can eat them there."

"Nanna probably has some, or some other cereal."

"No, she doesn't. She never buys Captain Crunch."

"She's shopping today. She'll buy you some."

"No, she won't because I didn't ask her to."

Frustrated, Aunt Julie said, "Oh, okay. Here." And put a box in the basket.

When they arrived at the check-out counter, Beth took a package of orange-flavored candies.

"Beth, put those back!"

Defiantly the child shook her head and held the candy close to her chest.

"Give those to me," said Aunt Julie.

"But I want them."

"You don't need any."

"But you always buy Betty some."

Giving up, her aunt said, "Okay, give them here. And don't ask for anything more!"

Beth, winning all the battles, ended up with three items that she wanted but did not need. Aunt Julie felt defeated, angry, and frustrated.

Beth learned that her aunt has a difficult time saying "no," and that she can be easily persuaded if Beth is persistent. Undoubtedly, Beth will continue this demanding, obnoxious pestering when she is with her aunt. In fact, since it worked so successfully, she will most likely try it with others as well.

It is a shame when adults teach children to beg, whine, and plead the way that Aunt Julie unintentionally taught Beth. There are many ways in which she could have helped her to behave more appropriately.

It is best to think ahead about potential trouble spots—though in this instance, an aunt may not be aware of what they might be. In this case, as soon as the child began to make demands, the adult needed to stop and deal with it. Aunt Julie could have explained to Beth why they came to the store, what they were going to get, how long it would take, and how she was expected to behave. At that point, she might offer a few suggestions and incentives for proper behavior. "If you can help me, we can go much faster, and on the way out, I will let you select one item at the check-out counter." Or, "If you will be helpful, we'll have more time and can stop at the library on the way home, and then read a story before lunch."

After these requests had been made clear, Aunt Julie should have ignored Beth's further pleadings. Her aunt might have told her that if she could not cooperate, the next time she would be left at home with a sitter.

When children make undue demands, they need adults who are able and willing to hold fast to the guidelines they have set, refuse to argue, and maintain a composed, pleasant, but firm attitude.

Fussing and Nagging Do No Good

Mother and Lisa had been arguing for months about Lisa's messy room. Mother had threatened, begged, fussed, and punished, but nothing seemed to work. Lisa's room got messier and messier. One morning Lisa was hurrying to get dressed, to go sell doughnuts for her Tri-Hi-Y. A friend of hers was picking her up in fifteen minutes. Her mother came in, took one look at her room, and announced to her that she could not leave the house until her room was cleaned up.

Lisa was furious. She yelled some obscenities to her mother and slammed her door. Mother left her alone.

Later, when the doorbell rang, Lisa came downstairs dressed and ready to leave with her friend. Mother called to her as she was leaving the house, "Is your room clean?" "Yes, it's clean!" Lisa yelled disgustedly back to her mother as she slammed the door and left.

Mother went upstairs and checked the room. The covers were thrown up over the bed, but there were clothes lying all over the floor, chairs, and desk. Nothing was cleaned up. Mother was disgusted and discouraged. Lisa had halfway made her bed and that was all. Mother closed Lisa's door and decided to "give up" on her room.

First, I'd like to say emphatically that nagging a teenager about her room does no good. Objections even fan the fire—by giving attention to the child for undesirable behavior. I think that a long, honest conversation with your teenager—where real issues are talked about and both sides are expressed and heard—would be a good place to start. Parents should be very honest about how they feel and what their expectations are. Then they should listen with an open mind to their teenager's version of things. Give her an opportunity to express her concerns, gripes, and wishes. Realize that as children grow, their needs change. It may be that she feels she deserves more freedom, less hassle about homework, or more privacy.

Then try some negotiations—make some deals. "If I promise not to hassle you anymore, will you agree to have the following chores completed by noon on Saturday?" "When you show me your completed list of chores on Saturday—then you will be free to make plans for the rest of the day with your friends." Of course the unspoken part of this agreement is that if the chores are not completed, the child is not permitted to go out.

Parents will need to be firm. They cannot afford to weaken or excuse the child in any way for not holding up her end of the bargain. Children will undoubtedly test you to see if you mean what you say. Be prepared for the child's anger at some point when she has not lived up to her agreement and lost out on the privilege of following through with her plans.

Sometimes our children have it too easy. They get everything they want with little effort. I feel we are doing them an injustice when we raise them to believe they are entitled to an easy life with little obligation on their part. They never gain an appreciation for the benefits of hard work and delayed gratification. When they grow up, they often have difficulty assuming responsibility and expect others to wait on them.

> Bud had been upsetting the other children in the fourth grade class all year with his use of dirty words and obscenities. The teacher had tried everything to make him stop using this offensive language. She had nagged, scolded, and fussed at him, tried to shame him, told his parents, made him sit alone, and given him extra work to do.
>
> On this particular day, Bud was at his worst. He had yelled obscenities out the window to an old man, talked back to the teacher, and made so many children angry with his insults that she decided she had had it. She took him to the principal and had him suspended for three days.

The children in the class were delighted that Bud had been punished. The next week he was back at school—up to his old tricks—using profane and offensive language.

Bud has learned how to get lots of attention from his peers, teachers, and parents with his use of foul language. The nagging, scolding, and reprimanding actually reinforced the behavior it was intended to stop. The child will continue this behavior as long as it gets the desired results. There are several alternatives that might help. The other children in the class should be encouraged to be unimpressed—to have deaf ears to Bud when he chooses to use dirty words.

If everyone suddenly began to ignore Bud when he used bad language, he might get worse at first, but then, most likely, he would quit trying. When he no longer received attention for misbehaving, he would put his energies elsewhere.

Parents fuss at their children when they are sloppy, inconsiderate, use the car too much, don't do their homework, expect hand-outs, and bring home bad grades. They think they can talk them into wanting to cooperate, and use words, threats, and fear of danger to try to evoke change in their behavior. Yet they recognize that they may as well be "talking to a brick wall."

Make Sure
that Privileges
Are Earned

Children are bored with our words and quickly build up an immunity to our fussing. Some develop excellent and successful coping strategies: they learn to look like they are listening or even go to great pains to cultivate a remorseful demeanor, because they realize that this has a calming effect on parents and cuts down on the length of the lecture. They may even go through the motions of temporarily obeying until the "heat is off," at which time they figure it is safe to return to their old ways. They have no real intention of changing their behavior because they have no reason to do so. When we do nothing but fuss at children, they continue to do as they please. They do not learn respect from this kind of treatment.

Parents need to learn to talk less and to act more. We need to learn how to back up what we say and let children suffer the consequences when they disobey. Some lessons are hard. Yet the earlier they are learned, the less suffering there will be in the long run. Just as a child does not run before he walks, he cannot stand straight until he has fallen and learned to pick himself up.

Parents have an easier job when they realize that it is their *actions* rather than their *words* that teach children respect for rules and order as well as respect for authority. Lucky is the child who learns his lessons early—not only will he be more secure and happy, he will be able to make productive rather than self-defeating choices and grow up to lead a more fruitful and rewarding life.

Questions and Answers

Q. *My eighteen-month-old throws a fit every time we change his diaper. He screams, kicks, and moves around so much that it is impossible to change him. I know that you aren't for smacking children, but that is the only thing that makes him stop. Do you have another solution?*

A. I know that this is a real nuisance. I would suggest that, instead of spanking him, you tell him that you will only change his diaper when he is still. If (and when) he protests, put him in his crib and leave the room, telling him firmly that you will come back when he is ready to behave nicely. As soon as he quiets down, go back and try again. If he starts up again, repeat the procedure. He will surely test you to see if you are going to be consistent. It will pay off if you are.

Q. *I have a terrible time getting my children to come home on time for supper. I have threatened, fussed, and told them many times how inconsiderate they were. After I have worked hard to prepare a nice meal, I feel that the least they can do is to be here to eat while it is hot. I hate to fuss, but I don't know what else to do.*

A. One way that has worked for other mothers is to tell the children that if they are in the house by 5:00, they may go back outside to play after supper, or watch TV, or use the phone. If they are not, they will have to stay in. Then stick to it! If they are five minutes late, they have lost the privilege. Don't weaken. Don't forget. If you will be very consistent, they will soon learn that things go better for them when they obey you, and they will!

Q. *How can I get my five-year-old daughter to come when I call her? She makes a game of it and runs the other way. It is exasperating and embarrassing.*

A. Tell her ahead of time what you expect (when you call, she is to answer you). Since she has gotten in a bad habit, it might help if you make a chart to help her remember. Each time she answers right away, she will receive a star on the chart. It takes five stars to watch her favorite TV show. Give her plenty of chances to earn stars. If she fails to answer, ignore it. Don't let her watch the show until she has earned the privilege. Don't fuss, scold, or get angry. Just make her obedience pay off. (When her bad habit is broken, you can discontinue the chart.)

Q. *My little girl, age nine, likes to wash the dishes. Every night she asks to do them, and if I tell her that she can do them if her homework is done, she gets mad because she hasn't finished her work. Then she balks and dawdles and ends up not doing her homework either.*

A. Perhaps you need to be more clear with her about your expectations. You could have a consistent agreement with her that she can do the dishes *if* her homework is completed before dinner. Telling her this only sometimes—whenever you think of it—makes her wonder each day if she can get by, and then she gets mad at you if you lower the boom. In other words, if these arrangements are agreed on ahead of time, and consistently upheld, she only has herself to blame if she doesn't live up to her end of the bargain.

Q. *When my children's friends come to our house, they often run through the house, put their feet on our furniture, set drinks on the coffee table, and do other things that we don't allow our own children to do. I don't know how to handle this. At times I resent the way they behave, but I'm afraid that if I complain, my children will be embarrassed and their friends will stop coming to our house.*

A. This can be a very touchy situation. I have always felt that in your own home, you have the right and the obligation to call the shots. In other words, I think that you should tell your guests what your rules are. Tell them that you want them to feel free to come there, but you have certain rules that are important to you.

Some teenagers would rather tell their friends what the rules are than to have the parents do it. If they are willing to do this, I think that is fine. I have found that when children know ahead of time what the expectations are and are dealt with openly and honestly, they are more willing to comply and cooperate.

Q. *Our son has a paper route, and he hates collecting his money from the customers. He keeps procrastinating, and when it is time to pay his bill, he often comes to us for help. It would be embarrassing to us for him not to have the money for his route manager, so we usually lend it to him. We can see the problem is getting worse, and we are uncertain as to our role.*

A. If you once lend him the money, he will expect you to continue lending it to him, and it will become easier and easier for him to procrastinate. Although it will be hard for you and perhaps painful for him, I would suggest that you tell him that you have helped him pay his bill for the last time. The next time he fails to have enough, he will have to tell the route manager himself and work out the arrangements with him. If you are lucky, the route manager won't like it and will insist that he be more responsible and dependable the next week. Hopefully this will be enough incentive for your son to hustle and begin his collecting early enough to meet his bill on time.

Suggestions For the Week

1. Make a list of age-appropriate behaviors for your child. Consult books, teachers, or other parents to discover what might be expected of children that age.

2. Take one behavior that annoys you and try the "When... Then" approach. In a casual manner, suggest to your child that "when he has... (emptied the dishwasher)... then he can (invite his friend to come over)."

3. Leave a note on the counter addressed to him: "When you have... (dusted the living room)... then you may... (go out to play)." Don't make mention of it. Preferably leave it before you go out, so that you won't have to listen to your child complain, gripe, or argue.

4. Make a list of the things you expect your child to do. Check yourself. Are they realistic? Age-appropriate? Are you prepared to follow through? Can you refrain from doing the job for him if he is lax or slow?

5. The next time you take your child anywhere, think ahead about the problems you might encounter. Discuss your expectations with him before you leave home. ("I know it's hard to sit through church. Why don't you take paper, pencil, and a magic marker with you to occupy your time? Try to see if you can remember things the preacher or Sunday School teacher says. Write each thing down, and I will play one game of checkers with you for each point you remembered.")

6. Anticipate temptations for your child and ward them off with counter-suggestions: "If you will sit quietly while we are at Aunt Peggy's, I will stop on the way home and let you swing in the park."

7. Have a family rap session the night before you need help with household chores. Tell the children what you need to get done and see how they think they can help. Encourage them to decide, calculate, divide up the work, negotiate. Don't criticize, offer alternate suggestions, or discourage them. Let *them* see if their plans work. Later, discuss how they felt, what worked, and what went wrong.

8. When you are going to take a child to the store, tell him ahead of time what you are willing and able to buy for him. Suggest that he can pick it out

when you are ready to leave the store, provided he has been helpful and well-mannered. (If he hasn't, leave without the present, saying nothing.)

9. Make a list of things you usually remind your children of and hang it on the refrigerator door. Keep a pencil handy and mark each time you remind (nag or fuss) about it or mention it.

10. Ask your child to tell you how he feels when you nag, complain, or fuss. Don't defend yourself. Listen.

Chapter Three

Stop Dangerous, Destructive, or Self-Defeating Behavior

The most tiring part of parenting seems to be the decision-making. Parents are called upon daily—hourly—to make decisions concerning their children. Children's behavior is often annoying, troublesome, ugly, dangerous, self-defeating, and destructive, and it is the parent's job to decide which actions to attend to and which to overlook.

It would be easier if we had some broad guidelines against which to measure our decisions—rules to help us decide quickly when to step in and when to stay out. I personally feel that we can learn to "tune out" misbehavior that is merely annoying or irksome. When we ignore it, it usually goes away.

But there are three kinds of occasions when I feel it is the adult's responsibility to intervene:

1. when the behavior is dangerous (to self or others);
2. when it is destructive; and

3. when it is self-defeating (any misbehavior that causes the child to lose face, or causes the parent embarrassment—which in turn affects the child's "likeable-ness").

It can be hard for parents to say "no." There is a tendency for many loving parents to be too permissive and to overlook behavior that they have every right to stop. Then when the behavior gets out of hand and they have reached the breaking point, they come down hard—in anger—and slap on punishment for something that could easily have been stopped earlier.

Behavior that is dangerous, destructive, or self-defeating needs to be addressed. When you decide to attend to the behavior, it needs to be done quickly, with as little attention as possible. The behavior needs to be stopped! Be consistent. Follow through.

A look may be all that's necessary. Nonverbal communication is great. You might look at the child and shake your head. If that doesn't work, then walk over to the child and take him by the hand. Hold his hand and say "stop it." Or take him by the hand and lead him to a private spot. Get down on your knees and look him straight in the face, and you know what will happen? Frequently he'll say, "I won't do it any more." Often you don't even need to discuss it further.

If that doesn't work, you may need to isolate him. You may need to have a time-out spot—a chair, or special rug. It's not a place where he is sent to be embarrassed or humiliated. The whole concept of "time-out" is that we all need an R & R location, a place where we can re-group. And you're saying to this child, "You need to re-group. You need to pull yourself together."

Sometimes I need to pull myself together. I need to say to my family, "I'll be back. I'm out of sorts, I'm out of laughs, I'll be back in ten minutes." And I come back much better off. And they're happy I left!

The time to deal with the problem itself is later—when the child has cooled off and has had time to think about it. Then you will both be more level-headed and better able to deal with the situation.

Later, when you deal with it, talk to him about what went wrong. Help him learn from the situation. "How can I best help you? How can I help you remember not to do that again? What do you think was wrong? How did you feel?" Get him to talk. Sometimes it's important to talk to the whole family. "What kind of rules can we really follow? What's important enough for us to have rules about?"

Children who do not have limits imposed on them when they are young find it difficult to impose limits on themselves when they get older. If we are consistent with our rules, eventually the child will internalize these controls and be able to stop *himself* when he is tempted to break them. He will grow up to be more secure, sociable, and productive because he knows how to put limits on himself and to exercise self-control when the external controls are no longer present.

Ignore Minor Misbehavior

> Stuart, nine, had begun rolling his eyes back until you could only see the whites, and then fluttering his eyelids. This drove his mother crazy.
>
> They were visiting a friend when he started to do it again. "Stuart, would you please stop rolling your eyes? It's driving me crazy. Stu-art! You're rolling your eyes again!"
>
> To her friend she said, "I just don't know what I'm going to do with Stuart if he doesn't quit rolling his eyes. Look, see how awful he looks when he rolls his eyes like that?"
>
> As usual, Stuart made very little comment to his mother when she reacted to his "rolled eyes." When asked to stop he replied, "Okay." However, he had a faint smile on his face after his mother reacted the way she did.

Stuart received a lot of attention for his strange and different behavior. Mother got "hyper," she brought it to the attention of her friends, and no doubt his nine-year-old buddies gave him much acclaim for his ability to produce such awful-looking eyes.

Children often "happen upon" little annoying habits (such as cracking knuckles, walking with eyes closed, burping, and making hissing noises). We need to decide which behaviors to cue into and which ones to ignore. It's my feeling that we can ignore about 95 percent of the behaviors that bother us. Learn to block them out. Walk away from the situation. If we are careful not to overreact—make a big deal of it—most likely these behaviors will disappear.

I went to a restaurant once with a friend of mine. Shortly after we ordered our meal, a fire alarm went off. A horrible sound. Nobody in the restaurant knew how to turn it off. We knew we had a choice: we could leave, or stay and hope that they could get it turned off. We were hungry, so we stayed. That noise went on for *thirty minutes,* and it was amazing how we could still carry on a conversation! That convinced me that we can tune out a lot of things.

You can tune out minor misbehavior if you try. This includes such things as arguing, silliness, whining, fussing, picky eating habits, getting dirty, spilling drinks, or deciding which clothes to wear. Even if you are in the car with children who are squabbling, you can look out the window, or turn the radio on. Learn the art of silence. Don't get yanked in.

Most parents feel compelled to put a stop to irritating behaviors. They either get mad and demand that the child stop, or become anxious and beg him to stop. They seem to think that if they don't intervene, he will carry this habit into adulthood. Their pessimism is unwarranted.

A child will persist with any behavior only as long as he is getting the reaction he wants. If he no longer receives it, he will figure it isn't worth his energy.

In the case mentioned above, if Stuart's mother had ignored his "rolled eyes" instead of carrying on about them, it wouldn't have taken him very long to figure out that this behavior gained him nothing.

If we are willing to change our reactions to our children's actions, we can make the happy discovery that drastic improvement in their behavior will follow.

> The family was seated in the pew at church with Susan, four, on one side of her father, and Stephen, ten, on the other. As the service progressed, Susan grew fidgety and began to slide around: standing up on the bench, crawling on the floor, stretching out and lying down on the pew. Each time the child moved in a new direction, Father quietly picked her up, straightened her out and sat her back down in the pew beside him. Father would look at her crossly or whisper loudly for her to "straighten up."
>
> Eventually Father tired of the whole process and picked his daughter up and held her in his arms during the rest of the service. Susan immediately became quiet and content, hugging and kissing him during the rest of the service.

Susan learned that she could gain her father's attention by fidgeting and misbehaving in church, and if she kept it up long enough, she could control her father even more—to the point of being held in his arms during the entire service. Stephen, meanwhile, learned that the way to get *no* attention was to behave and not cause any problems.

Susan's father could have ignored her fidgeting. Since it wasn't bothering anyone else, the child probably would have stopped if she hadn't received so much attention.

In addition, Father could have smiled at his son, or patted him on the leg to give him some recognition for behaving, indicating approval. Susan would have noticed the attention her brother was getting for behaving. Had she returned to appropriate behavior, Father could have been careful to give her a smile and a pat.

This father made the mistake many parents make: he gave attention to the child who misbehaved instead of the child who lived up to his expectations. We get much better results when we learn to reverse this procedure and reward appropriate behavior. Children will perform in the way that "pays off." In the long run, we will like our children better as they exhibit more age-appropriate behavior and they, in turn, will feel more confident, competent, and self-assured.

When Misbehavior Cannot Be Ignored— Stop It Immediately

Jimmy, four, was running around the reception hall tossing napkins in the air, spilling cookies, and bothering the guests. He filled his plate and ran down the social hall, tripping and spilling his food. He then ran right back and put more food on his plate, and ran again. The guests began to notice and some of the adults even tried to stop him, afraid he would fall or bump into someone. Their attention made him laugh and get wilder. Smaller children began to imitate him.

Jimmy's mother acted as if she didn't know him. By ignoring him, she was allowing him to continue his rude behavior, and he got worse. Eventually, when he became completely obnoxious and she was thoroughly embarrassed, she yanked him and shook him. She said in a very loud voice, "Don't you know how to behave? Go sit in a chair and eat like a civilized person."

Jimmy stopped running, but did not move toward the chair. Mother returned to her adult conversation, and Jimmy slowly returned to his shenanigans. Finally, after other guests were thoroughly disgusted, Mother decided to leave the reception hall and take Jimmy home. Everyone in the hall applauded when they left!

If a child tries to attract attention with minor misbehavior and gets none, he will probably stop trying. But when the behavior is dangerous, destructive, or self-defeating, or when he is getting a lot of attention, he needs to be stopped.

If Mother brings Jimmy to a wedding reception, she is responsible for him. By ignoring Jimmy's behavior, Mother was, in fact, sanctioning it. When children behave in certain ways in our presence and we don't stop them, they assume that all is well. In other words, the adult's permissiveness is interpreted by the child as approval. Research tells us that children are better behaved when *no* adult is present than when a permissive, non-attentive adult is nearby and does nothing.

The best time to stop an inappropriate behavior—when it is serious—is as soon as it begins. If we turn our backs, laugh, shrug our shoulders, or look the other way, we can expect the behavior to get worse.

> Mother had the play group—a group of five two-year-olds—at her house. The children were playing peacefully until Eric started hitting the others. Mother said, "No, Eric." He stopped momentarily. He started hitting again, so the mother said, "Don't hit people, Eric." Each time he was told, he stopped, but he always started up again.
>
> Eric hit the other children all morning. The mother scolded, reminded, and pleaded with him to stop it, but he paid no attention to her. By the end of two hours, she was exasperated and worn out.

Eric needed more than words. He needed action. This mother needed to follow through on her demands to Eric to stop hitting the other children. There are several things she could have done to convince Eric that she meant business.

Whenever he hit another child, she could focus all her attention on the hurt child and console him or her, ignoring Eric. (It is such a temptation to scold or punish the hitter, which often gives him the very attention he is seeking.) She could also try distracting Eric with other activities, and rewarding him whenever she saw him playing nicely.

If she was nearby when Eric hit another child, the mother could have taken his hands firmly in hers, stepped down and looked him straight in the eye and said, "People are not for hitting." She could have been very emphatic and held onto him until she was sure he got the message.

Eric should just not be allowed to continue hitting other children. If none of these techniques worked, he should be removed from the room. He could choose to come back when he felt like playing peacefully with the others. With a two-year-old, that would probably be quite soon. If he did not hit, then he could stay; if he did hit, he would have to be removed again.

It is not enough to tell a two-year-old to stop hitting. We have to follow up our words with actions—so that they know we mean business.

Set Limits and Be Consistent

Father had several very large plants in his newly carpeted living room. Pamela, two, was naturally attracted to the big plants and particularly liked digging in the dirt. There had been many times when Pamela dug in the dirt and poured it on her father's new carpet.

Father decided that the plants in the house were "off limits" and Pamela was just going to have to learn that. Father began to smack Pamela's hands when she played in the dirt. That didn't seem to faze her, so Father fussed and reprimanded her whenever she went near the pots.

Pamela didn't let the fussing stop her. She continued to play in the dirt and he continued to clean up the mess on the floor. At times, Pamela made a game of it, and headed for the plants when Father's attention was elsewhere.

Eventually Father gave away the plants.

It is important that children be given stimulating materials to play with—sandboxes, clay, paints—so that their curious natures won't get them into trouble. Children learn best through investigation: feeling, touching, seeing, tasting, and smelling. As muc[...] [...]ur homes, putting up most of the valuab[...] [...]ff-limits.

But children need not be given fu[...] [...]oundaries. If they do not understand the concept [...] [...]cure and uneasy, demanding and obnoxious.

Parents need to set limits and be consiste[...] [...]never the child steps over the limits, she needs to be treated in the same manner. It is wise to say "no" or "uh uh" *and* physically remove the child from the situation. Place her in a chair or other "time-out" spot and set the timer. Tell her that if she sits quietly, she may get up when the buzzer rings. This will teach her in a positive way that you are serious and that it pays to obey you.

If you are consistent, it won't be long before you will hear her say as she nears the plant, "no, no." Gradually, children internalize the restrictions we have placed upon them.

These are the roots of self-control and conscience—very important concepts for the young child to develop.

Fortunate is the child who has parents who are both able and willing to set limits and stick to them, for she will grow up secure in the knowledge that someone who is older and wiser will step in to stop her when her own judgment is immature, unsafe, or unwise.

> Mother had invited some of her former high school friends over to plan a class reunion. She had told Shannon and her three older brothers that they should stay out of the living room while her guests were there.
>
> Shannon insisted on coming in the room with the ladies, so Mother made an exception and allowed Shannon to stay, provided "she remain quiet." Shannon was loud and pesty and continually interrupted the guests. Mother kept reminding her that she would have to leave if she wasn't quiet, and finally demanded that she entertain herself quietly or leave the room immediately.
>
> Shannon then decided to color, and brought out her large tin box full of crayons. Mother told her that she could not empty them on the living room rug, but could use them in the family room if she wanted

to color. Shannon proceeded to dump the crayons on the living room rug.

"Shannon, what did I say about the crayons in the living room?"

Shannon said nothing. "Didn't I say not to dump them in here?" No answer. "Pick up the crayons and put them back in the box."

Shannon ignored her mother and kept coloring until the guests departed. Eventually Mother picked up the crayons after she had put Shannon to bed.

From this experience Shannon learned that Mother's rules apply to her brothers but not to her. She also learned that she did not have to obey her mother when there were guests in the home.

Mother will have a difficult time getting Shannon to obey her the next time she lays down rules. Shannon will expect to be an exception again, especially if there are other people around.

Children often become "mother-deaf" when words are not followed through with action. Shannon was probably testing her mother to see if she meant what she said.

If Mother decided that the children should stay out of the living room, she should have given them other alternatives and made it clear that she meant business. She could have told Shannon that she could choose to stay with her brothers in the den or play in her own room.

Then when Shannon first appeared in the living room, Mother should have removed her immediately and reminded her of her choices. If Shannon refused to stay with her brothers, Mother could have taken her to her bedroom and told her to stay there until she could make up her mind to obey. Although this would have taken more of Mother's time initially, it would have been worth it in the long run. Shannon would have learned that Mother meant business and her respect for her Mom would have been heightened.

During their family's week-long vacation at the beach, Amy, eight, and Barbara, three, had been allowed to extend their normal bedtime to 9:00. On this particular night, the household included nine relatives and two guests. Several of the adults, including both parents, were involved in a card game. At 9:00, the children were informed by their

mother that it was bedtime and they must tell everyone good night. They departed reluctantly.

After several minutes, Amy returned, complaining that Barbara wouldn't settle down and go to sleep. Their mother left the game to quiet them, while everyone waited. This procedure was repeated several times until finally she gave up and allowed both girls to rejoin everyone around the card table.

As time wore on, the children became fractious and cranky and were calmed only by sitting in laps, playing people's hands, and eating snacks. At 10:30, Mother finally forced them into the bedroom with the aid of a fly swatter.

The over-tired children left in tears, Mother felt awkward and embarrassed, and the other adults were disgusted and resentful.

These children learned that when other relatives and guests are present, they can not only extend their bedtime, but get attention upon demand.

Vacation-time can often be hard on children and the adults who care for them. Normal routines are usually interrupted, and adults, in the more carefree atmosphere, tend to relax the rules—when it is convenient. Then, when they are tired of the children's presence, they often come down hard and expect them to accept established routines without objection.

It's normal for children to push their limits—especially on special occasions or when they feel their parents are vulnerable. Successful parenting is not easy and cannot be accomplished haphazardly. Forethought should be given to potentially difficult situations and discussion ahead of time is helpful.

In the first place, it is unrealistic to think that an eight-year-old and a three-year-old should have the same bedtime. Naturally the older child will protest.

Special attention and time need to be given to children when they go to bed. Perhaps Mother could have let someone else play her hand while she attended to Barbara. Amy might have been allowed to stay up longer. Then, when the younger child was asleep, Mother could have excused herself again to see to the needs of her other daughter.

She might have told both girls that she would leave their doors open—so they could hear the adults' conversation—as long as they remained in bed and quiet.

By allowing them to control her, Mother was setting herself up for disobedience in the future. Children are happier, more secure and easier to manage when expectations are clear and limits are enforced.

Be Firm

Two-year-old Nancy's parents were going to a banquet. While waiting for friends to drive them there, Mother was giving the babysitter last-minute instructions.

Nancy was crying in Daddy's lap because she didn't want her parents to leave. Hugging her, Daddy reassured her that they'd be back soon.
Nancy got off her father's lap, down on the floor, and started screaming

and kicking her feet. Her father pulled her onto his lap and cuddled her. She kept on screaming.

Mother ignored Nancy and kept talking to the sitter. Daddy told his daughter that if she stopped crying, he'd bring her some candy. She stopped for a minute, but when she saw her mother getting ready to leave, she started again. This time, Daddy got mad and, picking her up, carried her to her room. As he was walking, he told her that now she couldn't watch TV. He put her in her room, turned off the lights, and closed the door. She screamed even louder.

Mother got upset and angrily told her husband that this was not the way to treat the problem. She opened the door and let Nancy out. She picked her up to soothe her and, at the same time, announced that she was not going out after all.

Nancy stopped crying immediately. Mother walked her friends to their car, apologizing for the change in plans, then walked back to the house, holding a smiling daughter by the hand.

Nancy learned that when she threw a tantrum, Daddy would cuddle her and Mother would rescue her. She also learned that she could manipulate her parents and get them to change their plans if she acted upset enough. In addition, she learned that Daddy's word wouldn't stick if Mother thought otherwise.

If Nancy's parents don't change their child-rearing practices, they are going to have a manipulative little tyrant on their hands.

They need to decide ahead of time when they are going out, and then stick with their decision. They should be firm—tell Nancy that she can cry if she chooses to, but she will have to cry in her room since they do not want to listen. She is free to come out whenever she chooses to stop crying.

They could leave a surprise snack or toy for her to find after they have left, or give her something special to keep for them (an old key ring) while they are gone. At any rate, they should hurry to leave and not allow her manipulative behavior to deter them.

One of the saddest things that happened in this case was Mother overriding her husband's decisions. If she thought that his punishment was too severe, she should have talked to him and tried to convince him to reconsider. By reversing his orders, she made him an ineffectual authority figure. Most spouses would resent this kind of interference and eventually either lose their confidence, or give up trying to take an active role in the rearing of their child.

Children who can successfully play one parent against the other are basically unhappy and insecure in the chaos they are allowed to create for themselves and those around them.

> It was Sunday morning, and Mother was getting her four-year-old daughter ready for Sunday School.
>
> "What would you like to wear, Samantha? You can choose any one of your dresses."
>
> Samantha protested. "But, Mother, I don't look pretty in dresses. I want to wear pants." She pulled her favorite pink pants out of the drawer.
>
> "No, Samantha, I want you to wear a dress to church. You *do* look pretty in them. Here, how about this one? Grandmother made it for you. You have always looked pretty in it. Remember?"
>
> "No, Mother. You don't understand. I want to look pretty. Don't you want me to look pretty? These pants make me look pretty."
>
> "Please, Samantha. All the other little girls in church will be wearing dresses. I'm sure Linda will wear a dress. The other mothers will think I don't care what you wear. Please choose one of these dresses."
>
> "No. I don't want to go at all if I can't wear pants. I'll just stay home. You want me to go to church, don't you?"
>
> "Oh, Samantha. I wish you would change your mind. Ple-ee-ze."
>
> By now Samantha had her pants on and was looking through her drawer for a shirt. "Here, how about this one? This one is pretty."
>
> "Oh, all right, you win. I guess it doesn't matter what you wear to church as long as you feel pretty." Mother reluctantly gave in.

Although Mother gave Samantha choices to make, the child made up her own mind about what to wear, and won the struggle for control.

This well-meaning parent is not doing her child any favors by giving in to her demands. The chances are great that Samantha will continue to challenge her mother's decisions.

This incident is typical of four-year-old behavior. Between the ages of two and five, most children are at times non-compliant and seemingly stubborn. They are unpredictable in that they may beg to do something one minute and refuse to do it ten minutes later.

The child of this age is struggling for autonomy and independent mastery of his world. Although it can be infuriating and baffling for adults, it is nevertheless a normal and necessary part of the child's development. He needs parents who can be firm, fair, and consistent.

A child needs to emerge from this period with a healthy balance of autonomy and cooperation and high self-esteem, but not so much power that he feels that he is a king and the whole world his subjects.

Spanking Is Not Necessary

While standing in line to buy tickets for the movie, Greg, six, became restless and started crying, "I don't feel good, and I don't want to wait in this stupid line to see a dumb movie."

"Shut up," reprimanded Daddy.

Greg kept crying and whining.

Snatching one of Greg's arms, his father slapped the child across the face.

Greg cried louder. His mother stood helplessly by, watching and saying nothing. Finally his sister Donna tried to console him.

"Leave him alone and let him cry," Daddy scolded his daughter.

By this time, other moviegoers were paying attention to the family incident. Embarrassed, Donna took her brother by the hand and walked with him outside.

This six-year-old boy learned that when he was tired or upset, it did no good to elicit help from his family. In fact, it angered his father to the extent that he hit him. He also learned that his mother would not rescue him. His sister seemed to be the only one sensitive to the fact that he was in trouble and needed to be removed from the situation.

Research tells us that when children are hit, their first impulse is to escape. If that is not possible, they become aggressive: fighting and hitting, or destroying what belongs to others. If neither of these outlets is possible, they will—as a last resort—turn their anger inward: becoming isolated, shy, retiring, and withdrawn.

When parents strike a child, it is difficult to know how it will affect him in the years to come. It is wise for us to realize that our actions *do* have long-term effects on our children's personalities. Therefore we should be careful to model caring, sensitive behavior, rather than resorting to impulsive outbursts that can be embarrassing and devastating to a child who needs us for love, support, and understanding.

Father and Carl were waiting in the airport lounge looking at magazines. Carl became restless and asked his father for a quarter so he could watch the small pay television set. Father told him "no," and to sit quietly until it was time to go. Carl started nagging and telling his father that a quarter was not much money. He became louder and louder, demanding the quarter.

He finally got so loud that Father became angry and slapped him. This made Carl cry even louder. Embarrassed, Father looked at the clock and gave him the quarter. He told him that he only had enough time for one show.

First of all, Father should have realized how bored Carl might become while waiting at the airport. If he had tried to divert his attention with a walk, a snack, or even conversation, he might not have become so restless. When he asked for the quarter, Dad should have decided right away whether or not he wanted him to have it. Waiting to make the decision until the boy's behavior was embarrassing him only made the problem worse.

A recent study revealed that 81 percent of U.S. parents used corporal punishment on their children during 1982. More than 60 percent spanked them at least once a week. Forty-six percent of college students surveyed revealed that they had been physically assaulted by a parent during their senior year in high school.

Obviously many loving parents spank their children, and many children who have been spanked turn out to be productive, well adjusted, self-controlled, and loving human beings. However, most parents do not like hitting their children and wish that there were other ways to insure success, respect, and trust. They only resort to physical punishment because they think it is necessary and are afraid that "sparing the rod" will, indeed, "spoil the child."

I feel that spanking children is not necessary. Of course, as I have said earlier, I am a firm believer in discipline. But I feel that there are more effective ways to help children develop internal control than by using external force. I believe that spanking is a poor method of dealing with children's misbehavior and, furthermore, can have dangerous or negative side effects. I would like to share some of these potential side effects with you:

- Spanking breeds hostility and anger. No one feels good about being hit.

- Spanking does not stop the unwanted behavior. Children are often tempted to repeat the behavior, out of spite, to see if they can get by with it.

- Spanking creates new problems. It introduces anger to the already existing problem.

- Spanking can lead to child abuse. Obviously, if children were never hit, our problem of physical child abuse would be virtually eliminated.

- Spanking can lead to neurotic behavior. Certain children become so upset and anxious that they develop defense mechanisms which prevent them from functioning normally.

- Spanking teaches that might makes right. Children learn that the way to solve problems is through violence.

- Spanking is a violation of the child's right. If the same injuries were inflicted on an adult, the aggressor could be charged with assault and battery.

- Spanking fails to teach appropriate behavior. The emphasis is on what *not* to do, rather than on what *to* do.

- Spanking interrupts the learning process. Children have to be in a receptive state of mind to learn. A child who has just been spanked is *not* in a receptive mood.

- Spanking leads to fear and avoidance. We even say to children, "Don't let me ever catch you doing that again." The child says to himself, "All right, I'll make sure that you don't catch me next time."

- Spanking makes the child want to strike or hit back. This is a natural, normal instinct—a defense mechanism with which we are born.

- Spanking blocks communication. We need to be in the business of building communication with children, not destroying it.

- "Not spanking" forces one to find alternatives to this form of discipline. It challenges us to use our minds to accomplish our goal: helping the child understand that the behavior is inappropriate and unacceptable.

- As the child grows older, the spanking must become more severe to be effective. A child of twelve will laugh at you if you swat him on the rear.

- The "spanker" becomes a model for aggression. The child will imitate this aggressive behavior on the next victim: neighbor, child, sibling, or dog.

- The spanking doesn't stop when the lesson is learned, it stops when the spank*er* is tired. The cessation of the act has nothing to do with the determination of the spank*ee* to change his ways.

- If more than one child is involved, the innocent one may be spanked. Most of us remember with bitterness some time in our childhood when we took the rap for someone else who got off "scot free."

- The child may "opt" to take a spanking and risk getting caught if his only reason for behaving is to escape punishment.

- Spanking does not lead to inner control. Children who rely on external controls to stop them grow up to be undisciplined, sneaky, unruly, unreliable, and defiant.

In a society that is becoming increasingly violent, it seems important that we try to find alternative, non-violent ways to solve our problems with children and to help them develop self-control without resorting to external force or physical punishment.

Questions and Answers

Q. *Our little girl, three, has developed a habit that scares me to death. Whenever she is angry, she lies on the sofa and gets stiff as a board, then closes her eyes and shakes. I have to beg and plead with her and rub her forehead before she'll stop.*

I have taken her to several doctors who ran tests on her and say there is nothing wrong with her. They tell me that she does this for attention and that I should ignore her. How can I ignore her? I'm afraid someday she'll pass out.

A. I would like to relay some advice passed along to me by one of my readers:

"Our little girl, age one year, began slapping herself when she was frustrated or couldn't have what she wanted. At first, it alarmed us and we said, 'No, baby. Stop. You'll hurt yourself.'

"She began slapping herself harder.

"Then we remembered your advice to ignore the behavior we wanted to go away, so we tried it. At first it was difficult and she slapped even harder and watched us closely for our reaction. We consistently looked the other way or left the room. Within a week, the behavior was nonexistent.

"We wonder how it would have turned out if we had continued to give it our undivided attention."

I would take the doctor's advice and ignore it. It would probably help if you leave the room and leave someone who is less emotionally attached in charge.

Q. *How can I stop my three-year-old from biting his little sister? He has also begun to bite his friends. My mother tells me to bite him back, but I can't bring myself to do that. Is there another way to stop him?*

A. Because we should model adult behavior to children and not stoop to imitate theirs, I am not in favor of biting children. However, it is imperative to stop a child from biting others. When he bites, tell him that you do not want him to bite. Speak in a calm, definite manner—"No biting." Remove him from the other child, holding him, if necessary, until you are sure that he knows what you mean. If he should repeat the biting as soon as he rejoins the others, remove him altogether for a longer period of time (restrict him to another corner of the room or room of the house—away from the action). If you are calm and consistent, he will get the message. He will learn that biting is "out of bounds" and that he loses the privilege of being with his friends (or sister) when he exhibits such behavior.

Q. *What do I do when my child runs in the street? I have been told that you do not advocate spanking. How else can I teach him not to go in the street?*

A. When you spank a child for running in the street, there is a danger that you teach him to look out for you and not for cars. It works must better to walk quickly after him, firmly take his hand, and bring him back to safety. Then get on your knee, look him in the eye, and say, "Don't go in the street." Hold his hand if he tries to return, or if necessary, take him in the house. Let him know you mean business.

Q. *Our two-year-old son Bernie doesn't like to wear clothes. In fact, he often takes his clothes off outdoors and runs around naked. I'm tired of chasing him and putting his clothes back on, so I have just allowed him to run around in the yard "bare bottom." Even in cold weather, he takes sweaters and coats off because he doesn't like to wear them. Our neighbors are upset by all of this. They have begun to talk and tell their children not to come into our yard. What do you think?*

A. We need to teach children that there is a time and a place for certain behavior. I would convey to him the message that for many reasons, it is not proper to go outside without clothes on. If he insists on taking them off, bring him inside and make him stay there (until he gets the message: no clothes, no outdoor play). Two-year-olds who have too much control over their parents often grow up to be unpopular, obnoxious, and insecure. Their self-esteem is enhanced when they know that there are limits to their behavior and that someone older and wiser cares enough about them to take the time and the energy to enforce those limits.

Q. *Our two-year-old has suddenly stopped eating. Meal times have become the most dreaded time of the day. I try everything—from fixing his favorite foods, spoon-feeding him, promising him dessert if he eats one biteful of everything, and sitting with him while he eats. Nothing works. I worry constantly about whether or not he is getting enough of the right foods. What can I do?*

A. Stop worrying. Put good foods in front of your two-year-old at meal time, and then look the other way. Show no interest in whether or not he eats. When the family is finished with their meal, remove the food that is left. Say nothing. Do *not* provide snacks of any kind before the next meal. When your child becomes hungry, he will eat, but he should learn that eating is to satisfy hunger, not to satisfy parents. Remember also that two-year-olds do not need to eat as much as they did six months earlier. Their high levels of energy and enthusiasm tell us, however, that they eat enough to nourish their bodies. If your son lacks energy and enthusiasm, check with your doctor.

Q. *I have a daughter who will soon be three, and she's not toilet trained. When I take her to the bathroom, she goes most of the time. Sometimes she realizes she is wetting her pants, and says she has got to go in her potty. Should I keep training pants or diapers on her? I get mad when she wets her pants and spank her, but she still wets.*

A. Toilet training often becomes a battleground with young children, but it is up to the parents to make sure that the child does not get attention and reinforcement for this non-accommodating behavior. It sounds as if your daughter is getting a lot of both.

I would suggest that you change your tactics completely. Tell her that from now on it is up to her whether or not she uses the potty. If she does, she may wear "big girl pants;" if she wets, she will wear diapers. I would put her diapers back on and use them, without any more lectures or fussing. If she insists on big girl pants, tell her you will try them in a few days. In other words, make her want to wear the pants. The minute she wets or has an accident, simply remove the pants and put the diapers back on. The less she hears about the subject, the better. I would not even discuss it with anyone else in front of her.

It sometimes helps to put diapers back on and tell the child that on her third birthday she may start wearing big girl pants. This often works. It convinces the child ahead of time that she will be able to control her functions and gives her an incentive for doing so.

Q. *When we go out to a restaurant, our son Billy, ten, always wants a steak. We can't afford a steak every time we go out, nor do we feel that he needs one. We get less expensive food for ourselves. However, he puts up such a fuss and refuses to eat anything if he can't have a steak, so we usually give in. Should we give up going out to dinner, or is there another answer to this problem?*

A. By all means, don't stop going out to eat because of Billy's demands. However, you should stop giving in to him. Explain ahead of time where you are going, and tell him what his choices will be. Tell him that he may not order a steak because it is too expensive. If he refuses to eat, let him go hungry. Don't give him anything to eat until the next meal. He may fuss, pout, complain, beg for food, or try other ways to make you feel guilty, but be strong. He will learn a valuable lesson if you stick to your guns—that he can no longer control you in public. After that, eating out with Billy will be a more pleasant experience.

Suggestions for the Week

1. Practice the art of silence. The next time your children argue, say nothing. If necessary, become involved in something else—read the newspaper or leave the room. Keep a notebook handy and give yourself a mark for each time that you remember. Record what happens next when the children bicker.

2. Offer limited choices. "You may wear either this dress or that one." Then stick to it. Treat arguments, complaints, and rebuttals with silence. (If the child actually defies you and starts to put on pants, calmly remove them, put them away and remind her that she must choose between the two dresses.)

3. Practice telling your child only once what you expect. Do not repeat yourself. Walk away. Act as if she will obey. "Go ahead and choose one. Then come to my room so I can help you button up."

4. Prepare the child ahead of time for any changes in the schedule. "In five minutes it will be time to clean up." "We are going to Aunt Margaret's for dinner tomorrow."

5. Practice rewarding the child for appropriate behavior. "It makes me happy to see how nicely you two have been playing together. I have time to play a game of cards with you now, because I have been able to get all of my work done faster than usual." Hug your child in church when he is sitting quietly and not disturbing anyone.

6. If you consider your child's behavior to be dangerous, destructive, self-defeating, or embarrassing to you, stop it immediately—with as little reinforcement as possible.

7. If the child persists in being negative, try "time-out." Remove the child from the situation temporarily, and have him sit in a certain chair until he is quiet and ready to cooperate.

8. Later, when the air is clear, explain to the child why you could not allow him to continue to behave in dangerous, destructive, or self-defeating ways. Help him to see his mistakes. Assure him that we all make mistakes, and that you want to help him learn from his and not repeat them.

Sensitive
Parenting

9. If you decide that you would like to try to stop spanking, talk with your child about it. Tell him why you have been spanking (because you thought it was necessary), and why you are going to try to stop (because you feel there are better ways to teach him what he needs to learn). Depending on the age of the child, ask him how he feels about discipline. What helps him to behave? How does he feel when he is spanked?

10. Decide ahead of time what you are going to do the next time misbehavior occurs. Have a plan of action—a substitute for spanking. Let the child know what he can expect: time-out, loss of privileges, living with consequences, and rewards for appropriate behavior. He will surely test you, at times, to see if you are serious. Be patient with yourself, and don't expect changes overnight.

Chapter Four

Reward Appropriate Behavior

Children repeat the behaviors that win them attention and eliminate those that don't. If babies are cared for by deaf parents, within three months they will stop making noise when they cry—they merely squirm, turn red, and shed tears. Because their crying does not bring a reward, they extinguish that behavior.

Since we all learn by trial and error, it is especially important that we make it worth the child's while to behave in ways that are productive, age-appropriate, and socially acceptable. We need to be very careful not to reward the behaviors we want to eliminate and to reward those that we wish to build upon.

It is frequently helpful to offer incentives when a child's misbehavior has become a habit—or when he has been receiving attention for the wrong behavior. Most of us respond favorably to incentives. We work harder when we are appreciated or noticed, or when we receive payment for our services. We tend to lose interest when there is no pay-off. Of course, it is ideal when the intrinsic reward is great enough to motivate us, but children are too young to have developed a strong sense of internal rewards. Gradually and eventually, the child's reward will become intrinsic, but I think it is unrealistic to expect that to happen very early.

Since behavior is learned, it can also be unlearned. I am referring to surface behavior—habits that we have developed or failed to develop. If an incentive program *doesn't* work, there can be several reasons: perhaps the incentive wasn't powerful or important enough, or it was used incorrectly (as a threat or punishment), or the need to exhibit that particular behavior was greater than the need for the reward. When an incentive doesn't work, a further look at the behavior, the reason for it, and the pay-off is warranted.

Any incentive system should follow these guidelines: first, it is necessary to isolate one behavior that you would like to change. It has to be one that can be measured (how many times a person has to be called to get up, or is late to breakfast, or completes her homework by a certain time, or makes her bed without being reminded.)

Then you must find an incentive that the person is willing to work for. Sometimes—in our affluent society—it is necessary to take away a privilege, and allow the child to earn it back. (Of course, she won't think much of that idea, but if the new habit is a behavior that you think is very necessary—such as completing her homework—it will be worth it.)

There can be short-term rewards (stickers, stars, or points on a chart), and long-term rewards (having a friend over to spend the night, going skating or to a movie). Once the reward system has been set up, the child should be left on her own to remember the bargain—with no reminders. When rewards have been earned, they should not be taken away. No reward is given unless the behavior is accomplished completely as agreed upon. No excuses should be allowed—even unavoidable circumstances such as sickness—but always make it possible for the child to continue getting rewards. Set up the program so that a long-term reward comes after five stickers, for example. Do not insist on five consecutive stickers, or one for every day of the week, because then if a child fails on Monday, she has no incentive to keep on trying.

I remember when I first began to jog. I hated every minute of it, so I needed a lot of encouragement. At first I carried mints in my pocket and ate one at the end of each block. Then I graduated to eating one after each half mile. Finally I left the mints on the kitchen counter and ate one when I finished jogging.

Realizing that eating candy was rather counter-productive, I changed my reinforcer: I asked my secretary and students to ask me each day whether or not I had run that morning. Then I would run so that I would be able to tell them "yes" when they asked. For years, this gimmick kept me running. Finally I realized that I no longer needed affirmation from outside, and I ran because I liked myself better when I did. Eventually the extrinsic reward had been replaced by an intrinsic one.

But this does not happen overnight, nor does it happen with young children. Many times they need a boost, so I think it is wise if we can come up with incentives that will help the child over a hump, break an old habit, or develop a new skill.

Don't Reward Misbehavior

Neil, five, went with his parents to visit friends. After a short time Neil became restless. Having no one to play with and nothing to do, he began nagging his mother. "Mom, let's go home."

Mother stopped her conversation to say to him, "Neil, we won't be staying too long. Please be nice."

Discouraged, Neil settled back in his chair. Ten minutes later, "Mom, when are we leaving?"

"Soon, Neil, soon."

For five more minutes, Neil was quiet. Then he interrupted his mother again. This time she became angry and told him to "sit down and be quiet—or else!"

Once more he obeyed, but shortly after he began mumbling. Finally he blurted out loudly, "I hate you!"

Mother got up out of her seat and smacked Neil on the leg. She yelled back at him, "Don't you talk to me that way!"

Neil began to cry. Mother called her husband, who was in another room, and the three of them left.

From this experience, Neil learned that the way to get what he wanted from his mother was to yell out in a very impolite way.

Some parents unconsciously train their children to be rude and obnoxious, because that is the only way they get attention and action.

To avoid this, Mother might have included Neil in her conversation occasionally, by calling attention to his patience and ability to entertain himself. She could have made a deal with him: "If you will wait quietly while we visit with our friends, we will stop by the ice cream store on the way home."

The needs of children cannot be ignored. They will make themselves known on way or another. The route they choose will be the one we decide to reinforce with our attention and time.

Mother had promised to take Diana, six, to the shopping mall to buy her some new school shoes. When they reached the store, Diana went directly to the display showing the most expensive, latest-fashion shoes. She picked up the pair she wanted and brought them to Mother.

When Mother looked at the price, she refused to buy them for Diana. She told her that they cost too much, and in a couple of months she would outgrow them anyway. Diana pleaded with her mother, claiming that these were the shoes all her friends were wearing.

Mother stood firm and refused to buy them. She suggested that they look at other, less expensive shoes. Diana became furious. She screamed at her mother that she hated her and that she never gave her what she wanted. She ran out of the store, leaving Mother embarrassed by her daughter's action.

Mother followed Diana down the mall. When she found her, she attempted to comfort her, but nothing helped. Finally, as a last resort, Mother gave in and told Diana that she would buy her the shoes she wanted. Diana's demeanor changed immediately. She became cheerful and happy. They went back to the shoe store and tried on the shoes. Diana got the ones she had wanted.

Diana learned that the way to get what she wanted was to scream, yell at her mother, and throw a fit. Mother felt angry that she had allowed Diana to control her and manipulate her into spending money against her better judgment.

By giving in to Diana's rude and ugly demands, Mother was reinforcing this kind of behavior and can expect to see it repeated in the future, whenever Diana doesn't get her way.

Unfortunately, this is a trap that many parents fall into. By not being able to reverse this cycle of behavior, they grow to dislike their children and their children grow to lack respect for their parents.

Once the disagreement arose in the shoe store, Mother could have refused to argue with her daughter, and suggested that they leave to discuss it in private. They could plan to come back at a later time. In this way, a public confrontation would have been avoided and the respect that Diana and her mother had for each other could have remained intact.

> Daddy was cleaning house and trying to get his four-year-old son (who was watching television) to do his chores. Philip saw an advertisement on television which showed a dish of strawberries and whipped cream. The child immediately decided he wanted some strawberries. He asked his father, and Daddy said he would go to the store later in the day to get some strawberries to be eaten as dessert after supper.
>
> This wasn't satisfactory to Philip and he kept demanding strawberries. He begged and cried until finally Daddy gave in and went to the store to buy some. When he got home, Daddy again told Philip to do his chores. Philip threw another temper tantrum saying he wanted to eat the strawberries first. Daddy gave in and let him have the strawberries.
>
> As a result, Daddy's work was interrupted, Philip never did his chores, and when it was time for supper, Philip refused to eat, saying he wasn't hungry.

When parents are tired and hassled, they sometimes lose confidence in their better judgment and allow themselves to be controlled by the whims and demands of their children.

In this case, Daddy had work to do and he wanted Philip to help. Instead of following through with his intentions, he allowed his son to have his way. Philip probably gained faith in his own ability and power to sidetrack Dad and learned that he can cry and beg for what he wants.

This case is further complicated by the fact that Philip got by without ever doing his chores. He probably learned another important lesson: that he can get out of doing his work if he will divert his father's attention by making additional demands.

Philip is training his father to obey him—instead of the other way around. If this pattern continues, Philip is well on his way to becoming a tyrant and a manipulator.

Parents need to think fast when their child asks for something. If they decide to grant the request, they would do well to say so immediately, rather than wait until the child pleads and protests. If they cannot decide in a hurry, they can say that they have to think about it and will let him know at a specific time (in ten minutes). This lets the child know that he does not have to keep asking—or begin begging.

The behavior of the child that occurs just before the granting of the request will be the type of behavior that occurs in the future when he desires something else. If we want children to get in the habit of throwing temper tantrums when they wish something, we should wait until they throw a temper tantrum before saying "yes." If, however, we want them to learn to ask politely, then we should indicate our consent (or denial) as soon after their initial request as possible.

When the parents have stated their decision in a friendly way ("We will go for strawberries after you have finished your chores") they should then withdraw from the conflict and remain friendly, calm, and firm.

Offer Incentives for Changing Behavior

Stuart ran outside to play, carelessly letting the screen door slam behind him. His dad called him to come back and shut the screen door correctly 100 times.

Stuart was furious. He came back reluctantly and cussed his father under his breath while he was opening and shutting the door 100 times.

Now when his dad isn't home, Stuart slams the door as hard as he can. Out of spite he also frequently leaves the door open when his father is home—as if to prove that being made to open and shut the door correctly didn't teach him a thing.

This is an example of a bad habit made worse by a parent trying to help. This is often the outcome when parents call attention to an annoying habit and purposely shame, humiliate, or anger the child in order to break it.

We have much better success with our children when we deal openly with problems and offer encouragement and incentives to help them break bad habits. For example, in the case mentioned, Dad might say to Stuart, "Son, it really bothers me for you to slam the door. Would you please try to remember to close it quietly." If the relationship is good, most children will respond positively to requests made in this manner, when the parent avoids accusing, shaming, blaming, insinuating, or generalizing.

However, if the habit is a long-standing one and the child can't seem to break it on his own, I feel it is helpful to offer him some incentives for doing so. "Each time you close the door quietly, you can put a point on this chart on the refrigerator door. When you have earned ten points, I will take you fishing with me." By the time Stuart has remembered the correct way to close the door ten times, his bad habit will probably be broken. If he slips, however, he could be encouraged to earn another ten points for a different reward.

Some people are bothered by offering rewards for appropriate behavior—feeling that children should know right from wrong and should not be "bribed" for doing right. By definition, "bribery" is giving a reward for performing an unethical act before the act has been executed. Appropriate behavior is certainly in no way unethical, and the reward is not given until after the act has been executed.

In addition, all behavior is learned: both inappropriate and appropriate. Children need loving parents who will take the time to teach, guide, and encourage them to behave in socially acceptable ways—for their *own* good. When children have acquired unacceptable behaviors, we need to help them unlearn these bad habits and learn others to take their place.

One of my students wanted her three-year-old daughter, Ellie, to stay in bed at night. The child had never wanted to go to bed. She could go on for hours getting back out, wanting a drink of water, another hug, *something.* The mother decided she would try the reward system, and let Ellie go with her to get stickers. She told Ellie she could put a sticker on her chart the next morning if

ELLIE'S BED TIME CHART

GOAL: TO STAY IN MY BED ONCE I'M TUCKED IN.

REWARD: GO TO THE AMUSEMENT PARK

MON.	TUES.	WED.	THURS.	FRI.	SAT.	SUN.
☆	☆	☆	☆	☆	☆	

she stayed in bed at night. The mother also—wisely—made tape recordings of herself reading the child's favorite bedtime stories. She told Ellie she could listen to the tapes while she stayed in bed. For the long-term reward, Mother allowed the child to choose some favorite places to go, which they wrote on slips of paper and put in a jar. Ellie could choose one whenever she accumulated five stickers.

The first night, the child cried for an hour. She finally said, "I don't even like stickers!" Her mother was about to cave in. It's often difficult to start, especially if you're a tender-hearted mother. (The first time I let my little one "cry it out"—instead of rocking her to sleep, she cried for an hour. And I ate a whole cake—piece by piece! The second night she cried for ten minutes. The third night she cried about 30 seconds; the fourth night she didn't cry at all.) Children can get over these humps, but the first time is the hardest.

The second night Ellie listened to the taped story, and called her mother to change the tape when it ran out. The next night, she was asleep before the first tape was finished. By the end of the project (which was about two months) Ellie was asking to go to bed!

Once the new behavior becomes a habit, the extrinsic reward is no longer necessary. The child has simply unlearned a bad habit and put a new habit in its place.

This is a positive way to help children "get off a bad track." Many times they need a little boost or a little encouragement to get them going. In other words, they need for it to be worth their while to put forth the effort to "unlearn" one way of behaving and substitute another, more desirable way.

Sometimes all that is needed is an inducement that acts as a reminder—that puts into their conscious minds the importance of changing their way of doing things. Once the new behavior has become a habit or brings about an intrinsic reward (I like myself better when I jog), the incentive is no longer needed.

It was 7:15 and Kathy, age six, had only half-finished eating her breakfast. She was still in her pajamas, and her school bus was due in fifteen minutes. Mother started fussing at Kathy, reminding her of the time, calling her slow and irresponsible, and threatening not to take her to

school if she missed the bus. Kathy momentarily hurried whenever her mother scolded her, but she soon returned to her previous slow pace.

By 7:25 Mother was dressing Kathy and fussing at the same time. She yanked her hair while she combed it, asking why she had to be cursed with a daughter like this. Kathy was on the verge of tears, deflated and angry and certainly in no mood to start her day.

Both Mother and Kathy heard the school bus go by. Once more, Kathy had missed it. Mother drove her to school without saying a word. Kathy sniffled a little when she got out of the car, but Mother was too upset and angry to even say good-bye. This incident had started the day off wrong for both of them.

Many families go through such rituals every morning—when a parent assumes the responsibility for the child's behavior. Children are perfectly capable of getting themselves up, dressed, and ready for school, though many a well-meaning parent denies the child the dignity of assuming responsibility for herself. In the preceding case, Kathy knew that her mother would get her ready for school, and she allowed her to do so.

Young children can often be motivated by incentives to get themselves up in the morning and ready for school. If Mother decided to change the daily ritual and make Kathy responsible for herself, it would be wise for them first to have a talk. Mother could explain to her daughter that she would no longer be responsible for getting her ready for school. They might buy an alarm clock and plan a way to select school clothes—maybe by picking them out the night before. Then Mother could help Kathy make a chart with rewards for different tasks completed: getting up on time, getting dressed, eating breakfast, brushing teeth, collecting books and lunch money. They could agree that she would get a point for each task completed by the time a buzzer went off. When she had accumulated a certain number of points, she would receive a reward (having a friend spend the night, a trip to the park, or lunch out with Mother).

	EAT BREAK-FAST	MAKE YOUR BED	GET DRESSED	BRUSH TEETH	COMB HAIR
MON.	☆	☆	☆	☆	☆
TUES.	☆	☆	☆		☆
WED.	☆		☆		
THURS.	☆	☆	☆	☆	☆
FRI.	☆		☆		☆

KATHY'S GET UP AND GET READY CHART

GOAL: TO HAVE A 6 YEAR OLD GIRL GET HERSELF READY FOR SCHOOL — MAKE HER BED, EAT BREAKFAST, GET DRESSED, BRUSH TEETH, AND COMB HAIR.

REWARD: TRIP TO PARK, SLUMBER PARTY, OR LUNCH OUT.

If Kathy sleeps through the alarm, allow her to suffer some unpleasant consequences—arrive at school late or stay home, whichever would be the least rewarding and the one that she would be least likely to want to repeat. Of course if she stays home, she should have an uneventful day, spent without extra privileges, TV, or special attention.

Parents need to take time to help their children become independent by training them and letting them know exactly what is expected. Otherwise they may learn the usefulness of being helpless and go through life letting others wait on them.

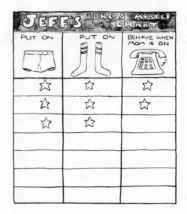

One of my students wanted to encourage her three-year-old son to put on his underpants and socks without help, and to have nice manners while she was on the telephone. She filled a drawer with toys that he could pull out and play with *only* when she was on the phone. She kept adding surprises to the drawer to make it more interesting.

Each time he put on his own clothes or cooperated when she was on the phone, he put a sticker on his chart. He had to fill up the whole chart before he got his reward, which was a Star Wars game. It worked. After a while, the child was into the habit of putting on his underpants and socks without help, and behaving while his mom was on the phone. He no longer needed the incentives.

Children who develop in healthy ways display an interest in doing things for themselves and delight in acquiring new skills. When we do for them what they can do for themselves, we rob them of the satisfaction and pride that come as a result of growing independence and self-sufficiency.

Reward
Appropriate
Behavior

When families implement such incentive systems, they usually feel better about themselves and have more energy to devote to positive interactions, which build—rather than destroy—self-esteem.

An incentive chart often works well with teenagers and their messy rooms. If there is something that the child has wanted (brand-name tennis shoes or jeans, a tape recorder, a digital clock—something that you would not ordinarily buy) they often are willing to "make a deal" and work for it. You could hang a chart on the inside of the bedroom door and set up a point system for daily chores: two for making the bed before going to school, one for picking clothes up off the floor, one for putting books away, five for dusting the room, five for vacuuming, etc. The child can record points at the end of each day and earn as many or as few as she wishes. The deal can be that when she has earned fifty points (more for a more expensive item), you will buy the desired reward. Once the chart is drawn up, no more comments are made about the room. Each night you can remind her to record her points—if she forgets.

Most children respond favorably to this method. They like the idea of no fussing, hassling, or scolding. They actually like being in charge of themselves, and it usually works—especially if the reward is something they really want and value, and will *not* receive otherwise. As they become more responsible, children usually develop a sense of pride about their rooms, and the rewards are no longer necessary.

A student of mine was very successful using this method with her seventeen-year-old daughter. The girl was willing to work for a new prom dress. The parents were so amazed when they saw that the system was working that they took polaroid pictures of her "new" room and invited neighbors in to see it! After the child had earned the dress, she asked if she might work for designer jeans. I saw the mother two years later, and she told me that the next year, when her daughter had gone away to college, her biggest complaint was her messy roommate!

These incentive systems do not work only for children. One of my graduate students decided that she wanted to change her own yelling behavior. She realized that her mother had always been a "yeller" and she had picked up that habit. When she announced at the dinner table that she was going to try to stop yelling, her daughter responded, "That'll be the day!" Of course, that made her even more determined. The family agreed to help her. As an incentive, they offered to cook dinner for her after she had gone five days without yelling. At first, she gave herself a sticker for each half-day she went without yelling, and when she had ten stickers, she gave herself a star. Whenever she received a star, that night her family cooked supper for her. She loved that reward, so it was enough to keep her motivated.

By the end of two months, she said that she had completely extinguished her yelling behavior. She then set up a similar program for herself in her classroom: she involved her students in reminding her and rewarding her for not yelling, and in another two weeks, she had changed her teaching tactics, becoming, for the first time, a soft-spoken teacher. Of course her school children modeled her newly acquired skill, and the noise level in the room decreased drastically.

My all-time favorite incentive program was used with an eighty-five-year-old grandmother in a nursing home. Her granddaughter was a graduate student in one of my classes. She told me that her family had put her grandmother in a nursing home. She was miserable—resentful because she didn't want to be there with all those "old people." As a result, she never went out of her room.

The granddaughter decided to try an incentive system, so she said to her grandmother, "If you will go out of your room for an hour each day and socialize in the nursing home, I'll let you put a sticker on a chart. For ten stickers, we'll take you out to dinner." The grandmother loved to go out—that was her favorite thing.

Every night the granddaughter's three-year-old son would call the grandmother and say, "Nanny, did you earn your sticker today?" And she would say "yes," and put her sticker on the chart that she kept. After ten days they all went out to eat. Then they started over again. By the time the grandmother had earned three trips out to dinner, she had become the social butterfly of the nursing home! Everybody there was asking her to come visit them, and she stayed out of her room much longer than an hour a day. And she was much better adjusted, for she was everybody's favorite!

Questions and Answers

Q. *My son, four, never wants to go shopping with us—unless we promise to buy him something. I hate for him to be so selfish, but I also hate to drag him with us against his will. He can certainly be a pain and a handful if he is miserable. Should I always promise a gift or not?*

A. It would be ideal, of course, if you could leave him home with someone else when he is unwilling to go. If this is not possible, I would talk very straight forwardly with him: tell him that you can't buy him something every time you go out (and don't let him talk you into it).

Make some deals with him. Promise him that your trip will only last until lunch time (or whatever) and stick to it. Promise some diversions along the way—a stop at the pet store or ice cream store—to break up the morning. Then suggest that when you get back home, if he has been cooperative, you will have a special "candle-light" lunch together. Be sure he understands ahead of time what kind of behavior you expect. Role-play the shopping trip and let him be the mother.

It is unwise to buy something for children each time we take them shopping. This can make them obnoxious and selfish, and we end up confused and resentful.

Q. *My five-year-old daughter expects me to play with her all day. I feel guilty if I want to read, knit, or even iron. She persists to the point that I usually give in and do my work when she is asleep. I don't feel that this is right, but I don't know how to change it. Any suggestions?*

A. I think it is very important for children to be able to entertain themselves and to know that other people have needs too.

I suggest that you make a deal with her. Tell her that you need some private time when she doesn't bother you. Set the timer for five minutes at first, and give her a sticker on a chart if she doesn't pester you during that time. Five stars will bring her a special treat.

Gradually increase the time to thirty minutes. Help her plan ahead with special toys or books to keep her occupied.

Q. *Our eight-year-old son has begun playing on a Little League baseball team. He loves it—but whenever he strikes out, he cries. It is embarrassing for him and for us. I overheard another mother in the stands making fun of him and saying that he had no business playing if he was going to cry whenever he struck out. Is there anything I can do to help him stop crying, or should we just ignore it?*

A. It is best for us to help children develop age-appropriate behaviors. I'm afraid that your son will sense the ridicule of others if he continues to cry whenever he makes a mistake.

Perhaps you could talk with him and tell him it is all right to cry—but it would be better if he could wait until he gets home. Give him a sticker chart and let him work for rewards each time he refrains from crying on the ball field. In the long run, he will feel better about himself, and others will not make fun of him, if he can learn to keep back his tears for a private time. Probably by the time he gets home, he will no longer need to cry.

Q. *My daughter, age twelve, bites her fingernails. She wants to stop because she is becoming embarrassed at the way her hands look. Her friends are beginning to use nail polish and she would like to have better-looking nails. Is there a way I can help her, or should I stay out of it?*

A. I would suggest a reward system—one that she would be happy with. Let me share with you a success story from a reader with a similar problem.

"Our daughter, age twelve-and-a-half, still sucked her thumb. She has braces on her teeth, and her orthodontist attributed the lack of progress to her thumb-sucking. Therefore it seemed imperative that she stop. She was not bothered by the habit, so this seemed to be *our* problem rather than hers.

We tried your suggestion. She had been wanting a pair of shoe skates, so we made an agreement and a chart. She could earn a point for each day she went without sucking her thumb, and when she had earned thirty points, we promised to buy her shoe skates. We were amazed—it worked! After a month, she was no longer sucking her thumb and we bought the skates."

Reward
Appropriate
Behavior

Q. *My daughter has told her son that in order to remain on the community basketball team he would have to make the honor roll. I disagree that she should use this as the "big stick." What do you think?*

A. I would much rather offer rewards for time spent studying than for grades. This would put the emphasis on hard work and effort. Grades are based too much on intangibles: ability, age, maturity of child, competition, and standards and personalities of individual teachers.

However, I also question the wisdom of using membership on a team as a weapon. Once he has made a commitment, I feel he owes it to the team to stick with it. This teaches lessons in responsibility and commitment, which are as important as good grades.

Q. *My daughter, age sixteen, wants to lose weight. She is very unhappy with herself and has begged me to help her. I try to fix the meals she needs, but she sneaks on the side. When I catch her, I scold her, and then she becomes angry with me. We end up in arguments and, for some reason, I feel responsible.*

A. Losing weight is hard, to say the least, and it can't be done by anyone except the person who owns the weight. It is such a personal matter that I feel it is dangerous for others to take on the burden of putting someone else "on a diet."

The only way that I have found to help another person is to offer some incentive if she wants to cooperate. This might be that she receives a point each day that she stays on her diet, or exercises, or eats fewer than 1000 calories, and when she accumulates five points, you will do her chores for her, or give her a dollar toward a bathing suit, or cook her favorite supper. A bigger reward for an accumulation of fifty points might be an added incentive. The last thing a dieter needs is a policeman, and no matter how much we would like to help, unfortunately, the work is hers to do.

Suggestions for the Week

1. Become an observer of yourself. Check yourself each time you look at, give attention to, fuss about, or mention behavior you don't like. Jot down on a note pad the number of times in one day that anyone in your home does it.

2. Practice "catching" your child when he is behaving appropriately. Reward him non-verbally. Walk toward him, wink at him, pat him on the shoulder, or hug him.

3. Tell a third party something positive your child did and be sure he overhears you.

4. Decide on one behavior you feel needs to be changed in your child—one that will make him more competent, responsible, or easier to live with. (Get himself ready for breakfast or the bus on time, practice the piano or feed the dog without being reminded, say something kind to his sister, stop slamming doors.) Keep a private record of the number of times in one week this behavior occurs or is a problem.

Then discuss it with him. Tell him why his present behavior bothers you and why you feel it is in his best interest to change. (Don't let his lack of enthusiasm deter you.)

Ask him what reward he would be willing to work for. Negotiate until you find one you can agree on and afford. Set up terms—a point for each success—and a long-term reward for a certain number of points. (Sometimes two long-term rewards are wise: your favorite dinner for every five points, and a skateboard for fifty.)

Help him make a chart, booklet, or poster on which to record progress or place stickers. Put it in a conspicuous place—if he wants to.

Don't remind him further of the plan. At the end of each day, you might ask him how he did, or if he needs help. Show an interest in adding stickers, points, etc. Don't mention failures—only successes. Never take away a point that has been earned.

Reward
Appropriate
Behavior

If the plan is not working after two weeks, renegotiate. Discuss why he feels it didn't work and see if he is willing to change the rewards and try again. If the plan is successful, change rewards and keep on going, until the habit is firmly established and rewards are no longer necessary.

5. Choose one behavior you would like to change in yourself. Tell your family about it. See if they will help by rewarding you in a certain way (breakfast in bed, cooking dinner, babysitting) and set up a similar incentive program for yourself.

Chapter Five

Let Children Solve Their Own Problems
(And Learn From Their Mistakes)

Parents need to stay in charge and set limits when the child is very young. But as the child grows and matures, the wise parent gradually lets go of the decision-making process and lets the child decide things for himself, and then learn from his mistakes.

It is important for us to be able to distinguish between a child's "wants" and his "needs." It is easy to confuse the two and treat them as though they are the same. Children resist growing up; it would be easier to remain a baby, dependent on others for care and support. When a child falls down, he may whimper for you to pick him up. However, if you give in to his demand, you convey the message that he really *does* need you to pick him up. In truth, he actually *needs* to convince himself that he is capable of picking himself up. If children have parents who cannot distinguish between their wants and needs, they raise dependent children who cannot make decisions for themselves and who will go through life unable to assume responsibility for their own lives—

trying to get others to make decisions for them and then blaming others if things don't work out.

As they grow, children also need to gain practice and expertise in communicating, arguing, standing up for themselves, negotiating, and compromising. One of the best places to learn these skills is right in the home—with brothers and sisters. Instead of allowing them the right to practice these skills, however, most parents interrupt, intervene, take sides, shame, or stop their children when they argue. For the most part, we would do well to extricate ourselves and let our children solve these problems themselves.

Parents should also encourage their children to think for themselves and to figure things out. "Do you think you need to wear a sweater today? Why don't you check the weather and decide." Even if you disagree with their decisions, if possible let them discover for themselves that it was a mistake. The best way to remember to wear a coat is to choose not to wear one and get cold. (I'll always go to football games prepared for cold weather since I nearly froze once at an Army-Navy football game many years ago.)

If a child forgets his lunch, let him go without. He won't forget it tomorrow. If you traipse to school and take it to him, "Oh, you forgot your lunch ... your lunch money ... your books ... your spelling paper," you convey to him the message, "I need to take care of you because you are not able to take care of yourself."

Distinguish Between the Child's Wants and Needs

Mother had been home with ten-month-old Jetty all day and was tired of giving in to her demands. She refused to entertain herself even for a minute.

Mother was looking forward to getting a break when Daddy came home from work. When her husband finally arrived, however, he announced that he was going to mow the grass. So Mother set the playpen on the patio and asked him to watch Jetty while she cooked dinner.

Jetty looked around, and seeing no one nearby, sat down heavily and began to fuss. Mother watched from the doorway. Daddy was busy getting the mower ready to cut the grass. "Jeff," she called to him, "help Jetty stand up."

"Nothing's wrong. She can stand up by herself," Jeff said from across the yard. "Stand up, Jetty. Stand up, honey." He continued working, without coming over to the patio. Jetty began to cry.

"Help her up. She's crying," Mother called.

Daddy ignored her and started the mower. Jetty cried louder.

Angry, Mother jerked the door open and went to the playpen. "Come on, Jetty. Daddy doesn't want you."

She took her daughter into the kitchen and gave her a cookie. She stopped crying.

Mother has confused her baby's wants and needs. Children need to learn to entertain themselves for certain periods of time and not be totally dependent upon another person to do it for them. This is necessary so that they will develop independence. When we run to assist the child every time she frets, we are conveying the message that it is a scary world out there and she needs help to cope with it. Instead, we need to teach the opposite message: that the child is able to handle times of being alone, and is perfectly capable of finding ways to make herself happy.

Mother is wearing herself out doing for her child what she should be doing for herself. Not only is Mother bound to feel resentful of her own time, but she is cheating her daughter out of the satisfaction and pleasure which come from growing independence—the right and heritage of all children.

Of course, it would have been nice if Daddy could have spent a few minutes with his daughter before he proceeded to mow the lawn. However, even if he chose not to, it would have been good for the father-child relationship if Mother had left matters in their hands and allowed them to work it out between them. If she continues to butt in, both father and daughter will allow her to continue to solve their problems for them. Unfortunately for all three, this invariably leads to dependency and resentment, instead of gratitude and security.

> Gary, two, was sitting in church with his mother and his friend, Clyde, seven. Both boys had brought toys to church. Soon after they sat down, Gary wanted to play with Clyde's truck. The older child was willing to trade.
>
> After church, Clyde asked for his truck back. Gary made a big fuss and began to cry. His mother asked Clyde if her son could keep the truck until they got outside, and promised to try to sneak it away from him later. However, when she tried to sneak it away, Gary cried even louder.
>
> "Oh, I'm sorry, Clyde. Could you let Gary keep your truck a while longer? He likes it so much. We'll bring it to your house this afternoon. Would you mind?"
>
> Clyde looked unhappy, but said, with hesitation, "Okay."
>
> "Thank you so much. You know how two-year-olds are." Mother responded as she picked up her son and carried him to the car. "I'll bring it to you when he takes his nap," she whispered over her shoulder as they were leaving.
>
> Gary, by fussing and crying, was allowed to keep a toy that didn't belong to him. His mother gave in to his unreasonable demands— thereby teaching him that it pays to complain and beg when you want something that doesn't belong to you.

Children need to learn that life can be painful and that we can't have everything we want. Mother needed to distinguish between Gary's wants and needs. He wanted to keep Clyde's truck, but he needed to learn that when you borrow something that belongs to another person you must give it back.

Parents must learn to tolerate their children's tears and unhappiness. They need to be able to look beyond the present moment and consider the best interest of the child and the long-term gains that can be made when a child learns that he can't have everything he wants.

If a child doesn't learn early on to tolerate unhappiness, he is destined for a lifetime of disappointments.

It was 8:30 p.m. when Carl, fourteen, came into the den where his mother was watching TV. "Mom, I need $6.50 to take to school tomorrow for school fees."

"I don't have $6.50, Carl. In fact, I don't have any money in the house. You should have told me sooner. It's too late now. I'm sorry."

"But Mom, I have to have the money. It was due a week ago, and my teacher has been hounding me to get it in. Tomorrow's the deadline."

"I'm sorry, Carl."

"Well, call Ginger across the street. She'll lend you the money. You know she will. She loaned you money last week for the paper boy, remember? Call her. C'mon, Mom."

"No, Carl. I'm not going to ask Ginger again. I'm embarrassed. She has a hard time too. You can call her if you want and ask her to lend you the money. But I'm not going to."

Mother got up and left the den. She went into her bedroom and locked the door.

Carl followed her to the room and tried to open the door. When he found it locked, he started kicking it. He hit and kicked for an hour, calling his mother ugly names and saying hurtful things like, "I know why Daddy moved out. You're so mean. How come you can always find money when *you* need it for something?"

After an hour, Mother had had all she could take. She opened the door and said, "Oh, all right, I'll call Ginger. You always get your way."

She went to the phone and called her neighbor. Shortly after, she left the house and returned with the money. She threw it down on the kitchen counter, with, "I hope you're satisfied."

Carl got his way. He learned once again that he could get his mother to obey him by kicking up a fuss and making her feel guilty.

It is sad when a child of fourteen is still throwing temper tantrums. Evidently he has been acting this way all his life because he has found that it works for him. His mother is a slave to his wishes and commands.

Most young children will throw a few tantrums in desperation, but whether or not they continue to throw them depends upon the way they are handled by the adults in charge. If the child receives attention (even negative attention), or worse yet, if the adults give in to the demands, he will keep using this method to get his way.

Some people continue throwing temper tantrums all their lives. As they grow older, tantrums take on different forms. Some adults become moody, quiet, or withdrawn. Others have fits (throw things, yell, break dishes, or speed down the street) while still others lash out—physically, verbally, or psychologically—against those they love. They continue using these methods of control because they have worked for them in the past.

The way to help someone change his action is by changing our reaction. Instead of giving in to his demands or altering our decision, it is best if we ignore the tantrum. If necessary, walk away, or leave the scene. As soon as he is over the tantrum and able to talk rationally about the situation, try to work out a compromise solution.

In the case mentioned above, Mother, by giving in, made it more likely that Carl will try the same method the next time she refuses to comply with his wishes. She had every right to be angry because he waited so long to tell her that he needed money. He had known it for a week.

She could have sympathized with his problem and helped him find ways to solve it. Giving in to his demands, however, did not help him in any way to become a more responsible person. I'm sure that Carl's mother felt manipulated and angry at his treatment of her. Parents need to gain skills early in their parenting careers to avoid problems like these.

In this case, Carl needed to assume the responsibility of solving his own problem. He could have learned a very important lesson by having to decide between going without the money or being brave enough to make the phone call himself. While he "wanted" his mom to solve his problem for him, he "needed" (for his own self esteem and growing independence) to solve it for himself.

Leave Sibling Arguments Alone

Father called the children to go with him to run some errands. As they came to the car, Diane was crying, saying that Matt had hit her. Father said, "Matt, you know better than to hit your little sister." Matt started to defend himself, and the fight was on.

Father lost his temper, ordered both of them to shut up, and spent the ten minutes it took to drive to the mall yelling at his children. His lecture included such statements as: "If you two want to fight, go ahead! Draw blood, kill each other. I don't care. But don't you dare come crying to me about it. I'm so sick of this fighting and tattling I could scream. Do you understand me?"

By the time they reached the mall, Father had a splitting headache and was feeling guilty for yelling at his children. They had lain down in the back seat of the car and gotten very quiet.

These children were accustomed to getting their father's attention when they fought. Without realizing it, many parents actually train their children to argue, bicker, and pick on each other. For example, one child provokes another child into an overt aggressive act, for which child number two gets blamed and perhaps punished. The first child is actually rewarded, then, for being the instigator of the problem. This leads to more resentment on the part of the second child, who will most likely begin to devise a way to retaliate. By interfering or intervening, parents are inadvertently teaching their children that "it pays to fight."

We need to reverse this procedure and teach our children that "it pays to get along." The best way to do this is to ignore children's squabbles and, instead, reward their cooperative behavior.

For example, this father could have said, "Look, you guys. If you will ride all the way to the mall with no fighting, hitting, or name-calling, I will give you a surprise when we get home. If either of you fights—no matter who started it or whose fault it is—*neither* of you will receive the surprise. Understand?"

This way father does not tell them how to work out their differences, but rather challenges them to get along peaceably. They are free to devise their own techniques for doing so.

Parents need to step out of conflicts and give the children room to work things out. If you are in a crowded space (a car), try to withdraw mentally from the conflict (refuse to react, turn on the radio, sing to yourself, or, if it becomes intolerable, pull off the road and stop—saying nothing). You will find that the fighting will diminish rapidly because your children will learn that it doesn't pay to fight.

When left alone to settle their differences, children establish far more fair and equal relationships than we can provide for them. They learn to develop equality, diplomacy, justice, fair play, consideration, and respect for each other—all qualities that are very much needed in later life.

> Jennifer, thirteen, had won a coloring book and crayons playing bingo. Her little sister, Paige, five, asked her if she could color in it.
>
> "No, I want to color in it first. I won it, and it's mine."
>
> Paige turned to her mother, "Mom, Jennifer won't let me color in her book."
>
> "Why won't you let Paige color in it? You're too old for a coloring book anyway," her mother retorted.
>
> "It's mine. I won it. Besides, I told her she could color in it after I have."
>
> Paige started whining, "I want to color. I want to color now!"

"Let her have it. I'm ashamed of you. It's not worth anything anyway."

"She always gets anything she wants. She's not gonna get this," Jennifer held her ground.

Mother was angry. Starting toward her and raising her voice, she yelled, "All right, young lady. You heard what I said. Give it to her now!"

Jennifer threw the book and crayons at her mother. "Here! I hate you!"

Coming in from the other room, Father overheard this last statement. "Shut up. Go to your room! I don't want to see you anymore tonight!"

After Jennifer left, Paige took the coloring book and colored a few messy strokes. She left the book and crayons scattered on the table.

Mother chalked it up to "those terrible teens," and father smiled with the assurance that he had solved the problem—because it was no longer present.

This way of handling the situation brought nothing positive to either child, nor to the relationship between them. Much was lost by the parents taking over the problem and making it theirs.

They certainly showed partiality by forcing Jennifer to give in to the undue demands of her little sister. The property clearly belonged to the older child and it should have been up to her to decide whether or not her little sister could have it.

If the two sisters had been left to settle the dispute between them, they probably would have worked out a compromise that would have been mutually satisfying. Paige needed to learn to respect her sister's belongings and to learn that she cannot have everything she wants. Jennifer needed to be treated with respect. The girls needed the experience of learning to settle their differences, and understanding for themselves the meaning of give and take.

It is in our families that we learn how to negotiate, bargain, debate, argue, defend our rights, stand up for ourselves, and respect the property of others. If parents do not allow their children to learn these valuable lessons, they grow up unprepared for and uncomfortable with conflict when it arises later in work and marriage.

After fixing snacks in the kitchen, the boys brought their food in the family room to eat while they watched TV.

"Someone left the light on in the kitchen," Dad reminded them.

"Marc, turn the light off," David told his brother.

"Turn it off yourself. You turned it on."

"You were the last one in the kitchen, dummy. The last one out turns it off."

"Uh uh. The one who turns it on turns it off."

"Dad, Marc won't turn the light off."

"Turn the light off, Son."

"He was the last one out. He should have to turn it off."

"I said, 'turn it off' Marc. Now do as you're told," Dad laid down the law.

Marc got up reluctantly and started toward the kitchen, kicking David's chair as he passed by.

"Hey, cut it out, man," David said as he reached in the air trying to swat at Marc.

Because Dad stopped the argument with his arbitrary decision, the boys were not given the opportunity to settle their own differences. Chances are that they remained angry with each other, and Marc felt resentful because he got the raw end of the deal.

This kind of bickering goes on in most households. The way it is handled largely determines the extent to which it is perpetuated. Parents worry whether they should step in or stay out of their children's quarrels.

Sibling arguing has been with us since Cain and Abel. It is difficult to determine how it began or how to make it end. It can be a valuable and constructive learning experience, but it can also be cruel and destructive.

Some bickering is brought on by fatigue, boredom, sickness, or hunger. If the immediate cause is eliminated, the quarreling will cease.

Other bickering is more constructive in nature—that is, the debating of issues. It can be helpful for children to have opportunities to use their knowledge and logic to try to persuade others. These discussions can be mutually beneficial and provide valuable experience. Children need to learn to stand up for themselves and their ideas and to disagree without attacking another's character.

As a general rule, however, children's arguments will be resolved more quickly if parents stay out of them. By intervening, we deprive them of a valuable learning experience and imply that they are not able to handle the situation.

> Peggy, seventeen, and Paula, fourteen, were the same size, so they could easily wear each other's clothes. Peggy was careful with her sister's clothes, and when she borrowed any, she always put them back as she found them.
>
> Paula was careless with Peggy's clothes, however, and frequently failed to hang them up, wash them, or sometimes even return them.
>
> On this particular school morning, Paula went into Peggy's closet and took a blouse off the hanger to wear. When Peggy saw her she said, "You can't wear my blouse. In fact, I've decided I don't want to swap clothes anymore, because you mess them up and don't return them, and I can never find what I want."
>
> Paula told Peggy that she was selfish for not sharing her clothes and went to tell Mother. Mother agreed that Peggy was selfish and told her she would have to let Paula wear her blouse.
>
> Paula went off to school wearing Peggy's blouse (smiling to herself), and Peggy left feeling cheated and angry.

Mother could have stayed out of this and let Peggy and Paula settle it. She might have offered to help them and suggested ways they could reach a compromise. A simple chart with "item borrowed," "date borrowed," "date returned," might be enough. No item could be borrowed until the last one had been returned. If the girls could reach a peaceable solution, each would feel better about the other. By stepping in and settling the disagreement herself, Mother probably helped to weaken the relationship between the two girls instead of strengthen it.

Consequences Teach Responsibility

> Answering a knock on the door, Mother discovered Richie, covered with mud from head to toe. He had been playing football with the neighbors.
>
> "Richie, what in the world have you been doing? You're done for the night! Put your bike away and get into the house!"
>
> Richie became angry and began to stomp away.
>
> "Wait just a minute, young man," she shouted, and she called to her husband, "Come here, Rich. Just look at your son and tell me what I should have said."

"Richie, your mother's right. You're done for tonight, and tomorrow night, too! That's uncalled for. You know better than to get so dirty."

Mother intervened, "No, he doesn't have to be punished for tomorrow night, too. That's too much. But you are done for tonight. Richie, go get your bike and come inside."

Richie stalked off down the steps and Mother closed the door.

Richie was angry with both parents and they were mad at each other. His father resented the fact that Mother had called him in on the situation and then dismissed his authority in front of their son. All three stayed at odds with each other throughout the evening.

The problem of the dirty football clothes was never solved. The only lesson learned was probably learned by Richie, who most likely will decide not to come home early the next time his clothes are messed up, since he would be made to stay home.

I think parents need to help children learn how to take responsibility for their own actions. In this case, Mother could have said, "Boy, you've had quite a game of football! You'd better take off as many clothes as possible in the wash room. After you've had a chance to clean up, you can get the mud off your shoes and wash everything in one load." If she was angry, she could have expressed her feelings about the situation and said, "Richie, I'm upset over all this mud because I'm tired, and I don't need another load of clothes to wash. It will be up to you to take care of your muddy clothes and shoes."

When parents take on the role of servants to their children, no one profits. The parents resent the extra workload caused by the normal activities of children and begin to resent the child. The child feels this resentment and retaliates with apathy and an "I don't care" attitude. Most importantly, the child fails to learn to accept responsibility for his own actions and doesn't develop the necessary skills for taking care of himself. A very important step in his development is overlooked.

If Richie had been taught at an early age that he must face the consequences of his actions, he would have been in the habit of thinking before he acted: "If I get dirty, I will have to wash the clothes and shoes." Then he would have had a decision to make—whether or not it was worth it. If he did choose to go ahead and get dirty, he would have known what he had to do when he got home.

Neither his mother nor his dad would have to become involved, and their relationship would not have been affected. Judgments and punishments would have been unnecessary and the evening would have been saved. Unfortunately, many parents use their energies in unnecessary ways, and then don't have any left to spend on actively loving, caring, and playing together.

> Buffy and Jeanie had spent the day at the pool. Buffy's mother had come to pick them up and told them to hurry. They went in the bathroom to change, and started playing around. They wadded up toilet paper, and, after wetting it in the sink, threw it up on the ceiling. Naturally it stuck there. They thought that was hilarious, so they repeated the process. Soon they were not only throwing it on the ceiling, they were throwing it on the mirrors, the walls, and the door. They were having a marvelous time when Buffy's mother walked into the bathroom and caught them.
>
> She grabbed her daughter by the arm, scratching her skin with her long fingernails. She dragged her out of the dressing room, saying, "I told you I was in a hurry, and here you are making a mess in the bathroom. Now come on and get your things. I'm going to drive the car around."
>
> While Mother went to get the car, both girls sat on the curb, giggling. Buffy imitated her mother's grasp and tone of voice, and both girls laughed hysterically.
>
> As a result, the girls got away with their destructive behavior and Mother did nothing about it.

Mother's pinching did nothing to correct Buffy's behavior. In fact, it was so ineffective that it made the girls laugh. They certainly did not receive the message that they needed to make amends for their misbehavior in any way.

Mother had every right to be angry at the girls for holding her up, but more than that, she had an obligation to hold them responsible for their actions. This could have been done in several ways: first, Mother could have told them how their behavior affected her: "When you mess up property that belongs to someone else, I am embarrassed and angry." Then she could have told the girls that she expected them to clean up the bathroom—right away and quickly—while she waited for them. Or she could have told them that she would have to leave and come back for them later. By the time she returned, she expected the bathroom to be clean. She might have asked them to go to the pool manager and tell him what they had done. Since most pools have rules covering the care of property, they probably would have lost some of their privileges for awhile.

Parents cannot afford to overlook the mistakes and misbehavior of children when they are dangerous or destructive. Since Mother had assumed responsibility for giving Buffy's friend a ride home, she had every right to demand that both girls make amends. In fact, by not doing so, she was sanctioning their behavior.

Of course, children will get carried away—especially when they are with their peers. As adults we need to stay tuned in to their behavior as much as possible, and put a stop to that which is unacceptable.

It would have helped the girls' future development if Mother had made them realize that they had no right to mess up property that belonged to others and to cause work for someone else. By reporting what they had done and by cleaning it up themselves, the chances are greater that they would become more thoughtful in the future and think twice before they made trouble for others or extra work for themselves.

> The family was going to the mountains for a vacation. Dana was driving on the interstate. His father and mother took turns telling him that he was driving too fast. He made some smart remarks under his breath and slowed up temporarily. Gradually, he accelerated again.
>
> A police radar caught him going 75 m.p.h. When he got in the car and resumed his driving, his father asked him if he could mail in the fine or if he had to appear in court.
>
> Dana snapped, "How do I know? I just wanted to get out of there."
>
> Both parents told Dana that he should have asked the officer what he had to do. They read the ticket and found that he was to appear in court on a given day. They were upset.
>
> When they arrived home, Dana's father called the police station in the county where Dana had received the ticket. He found that the fine

could be paid ahead of time. He wrote a check and mailed it in with Dana's ticket.

Dana's parents were allowing him to speed even though they told him to stop. Then his dad made it his business to call, investigate the proper procedures, and send in the money. In no way did Dana suffer for his errors—or learn from his mistakes.

Until he is forced to pay for the consequences of his actions, he will probably continue to break the law and get tickets.

Some children have parents who refuse to be parents, who refuse to stand for anything, or to teach their children the difference between right and wrong. They refuse to place restrictions on their use of cars or other possessions. Children who know no limits get very nervous. Many of them are looking for a way out—through alcohol, drugs, sex, and even suicide. Parents need to stand firm and make their expectations clear. Then they need to back up their words with action and let children learn from suffering the consequences of their actions.

> Bernie had just celebrated his sixth birthday, and he had received five dollars from his grandmother. His parents told him that he should save $4.50 of it, but he could spend fifty cents any way he wanted.
>
> He asked his dad if he would take him to the store where he could choose something.
>
> Bernie was excited. He walked into the store holding his head high, eagerly grasping the two quarters. He found the toy counter and slowly began his search. He was thoroughly enjoying his indecision and power. He considered many different items.
>
> Dad grew impatient and began to make suggestions. Feeling pressured, Bernie finally announced that he had made his decision. He wanted to buy twenty-five pieces of bubble gum—all colors.
>
> Bernie's father belittled his decision. He told him that bubble gum was bad for his teeth and a waste of money. He told him to pick something else.
>
> "Here, why don't you buy this truck? You like trucks."
>
> Reluctantly, Bernie picked up the truck and paid the cashier. As he walked out the door, his shoulders were slumped and his expression was clearly less confident and proud.

As they got in the car, Bernie threw his unopened package into the back seat.

Although his parents had told him that he could choose how to spend the fifty cents, his dad reversed the decision when he told Bernie that he could not buy bubble gum. Bernie lost interest when the decision was made for him.

Even though his father's judgment was more farsighted, Bernie was deprived of an opportunity to learn for himself.

Children need practice in making decisions. They have an inner drive to be independent and resourceful; when we make their decisions for them, we deprive them of a sense of accomplishment and control. We also reinforce their dependency on us.

Only by trial and error can children develop an accurate sense of right and wrong, good and bad. This doesn't mean that we should let them do whatever they please. It simply means that we should, as early as possible, give them many opportunities to make choices. In this way, we are helping them to confidently make intelligent decisions.

It is not possible for adults to inject values into their children. Children not only have to develop their own, they also have to learn how to make choices that are compatible with those values. This ability develops slowly—from within—with much practice, and some failures along the way.

By not allowing children to make mistakes and suffer the consequences, we cheat them out of many worthwhile experiences. If we undermine their decisions, they will never learn how to make them. Then, when they leave home for the first time, they may misuse and abuse their freedom and recklessly make irresponsible decisions that could affect their lives in irreversible ways.

> Arthur and Greg (age seven) were playing outside with a group of other children. Their play gradually degenerated into a conflict and, finally, open warfare. During the battle, a rock was thrown—hitting Greg in the chest, causing an abrasion and a bruise. He ran home crying, and a few minutes later, he and his father showed up at Arthur's door, demanding to see Arthur *and* his mother. His father did most of the talking—declaring that Arthur had thrown the rock that hit Greg and demanding that Arthur be severely punished.

Mother, intimidated by the size and anger of Mr. Clark, was horrified to think her son had committed such a crime. She immediately flew at Arthur, screaming that he could have killed someone. In front of Mr. Clark and Greg, she beat him five or six times with a belt and sent him to his room.

Mother took matters into her own hands instead of allowing her son to learn from the experience. He was deprived of a valuable lesson—that of resolving conflicts.

Mr. Clark and Greg were satisfied. Arthur sat in his room the rest of the day, crying, feeling humiliated and embarrassed—determined never to speak to Mr. Clark or play with Greg again. This was the beginning of a silent war between the two families.

Mother was upset that she had allowed herself to be pressured into a course of action based on the fear that her neighbor would think she was a weak and ineffectual parent. She realized that she had never given Arthur a chance to speak on his own behalf and had taken Mr. Clark's word for an event that neither of them had seen.

Arthur's self-esteem was undoubtedly lowered by Mother's treatment. His needs and opinions were discounted, which would certainly weaken his trust in his mom and her support. He was proclaimed guilty without being allowed to prove his innocence. Mother had allowed Mr. Clark to intimidate her into doing something to her son that was against her better judgment. Her relationship with Arthur certainly suffered a setback.

It would have been better for the parents to stay out of this conflict. When we make adult issues out of children's problems, we often run the risk of making them bigger than necessary and causing them to last for an inappropriate length of time.

Jonathan and Mark, both age ten, came to church school early, and were in the classroom before the teacher arrived. Bored, they started roughhousing, and Jonathan accidentally knocked Mark into a table. The table—which was being used to store clay items that the class had made for a project—fell over, and several of the clay items were broken. The boys were flustered and ran out of the classroom.

When they returned some minutes later, they found the teacher and other class members very angry. Many were speculating as to how the clay items had been broken.

Jonathan and Mark decided to confess. They told the teacher what had happened and stressed the fact that it had been an accident.

The teacher was furious. Without waiting for them to explain further, she hastily decided their fate: Jonathan and Mark could not go with the class on a skating party the next weekend.

Having looked forward to the party for weeks, the boys were crushed. They begged for another "punishment," but the teacher stood firm.

The boys felt that they had been mistreated. Once they realized that the teacher was not going to budge in her decision, they became sullen and uncooperative.

In effect, these boys were punished for telling the truth. They had been faced with a moral dilemma and showed character by choosing to confess. Even though the teacher was understandably disappointed and angry, there were ways in which she could have handled the situation that might not have alienated the boys and that would have helped them progress in their moral development.

At ten, these boys are certainly old enough to have realized that their actions would have consequences. They should have been commended for choosing to tell the truth in the face of probable punishment. The teacher could have accepted their explanation, realizing that accidents happen. She might encourage the boys to consider what they would do differently the next time they arrived early or were without supervision.

She could have suggested that they figure out a way to make amends. They might have chosen to repair the damage, or replace the broken items. They might have chosen to earn some extra money to pay for them.

The punishment chosen by the teacher was in no way related to the misdeed. I don't see how the boys could have learned anything positive from the way it was handled.

The chances are great that the next time these boys are faced with a similar moral decision, they may be less willing to be truthful.

When adults find it necessary to discipline (teach and train), they should focus on the *future* and decide what it is they want the child to do the next time he finds himself in a similar situation. Adults should make certain that the techniques they use will help children become more self-disciplined, independent, and competent citizens for tomorrow.

Jeanette had been dating Bob, who was three years older, ever since she was sixteen. Her parents had objected to this relationship, and with good reason: Bob had been in trouble with the law, had introduced Jeanette to drugs, and had been the source of many hours of depression, unhappiness, and uncertainty for their daughter. Besides that, he was the only boy she had ever dated.

On several occasions, Jeanette's parents had forbidden her to see Bob any more, only to discover later that she had found ways to be with him on the sly. They made their objections about Bob loud and clear, constantly pointing out his weaknesses and flaws, and threatening Jeanette with restrictions and punishments for continuing to see him.

When Bob called on the phone, they lied to him and told him she wasn't there. When he came to the house, they treated him with coldness and indifference. They refused to have him join the family for celebrations or trips, and demanded that Jeanette not speak to him again.

When Jeanette graduated from high school, she ran away with Bob and got married. Two years later they were divorced.

Unfortunately, Jeanette and Bob's story is not uncommon. Sad, but not unusual. At sixteen, young people need to begin to separate from their families and form their own identities. In an effort to do this, they are often attracted to other people who have traits they admire and/or who give them the feeling of importance they need.

The way this is handled by parents is important. They can "push" a child into a commitment she is in no way ready to make by punishing, laying down laws, forbidding the relationship, criticizing, and threatening. Although they had her best interests at heart, Jeanette's parents probably forced her to make a choice for which she was in no way prepared.

Parents need to exercise wisdom, good judgment, and understanding. They can best do this by helping the child "work through" her needs, and by providing her with the chance to do so. In fact, it is often wise to handle the situation in the opposite way from that of Jeanette's parents. Jeanette needed to know *more* about what kind of person Bob really was. Her parents could have encouraged Bob to eat with them and spend time in their home, hoping that eventually Jeanette would see the negative side of his personality and would tire of him. This would also eliminate the element of excitement in the relationship which the parents were causing by making it so difficult for the couple to see each other.

It is fine for parents to express their concerns and doubts, but this must be done gradually and tactfully, so as not to make the child defensive and determined to prove them wrong.

Teenagers need help, support, love, and understanding. If this support is taken away at home, they will seek it elsewhere and lean heavily on anyone who has it to give.

Children must learn from their mistakes, like the rest of us. But if parents are willing to give up some of their control, keep the lines of communication open, and still make their expectations clear and reasonable, the mistakes their children make will not have to be so drastic, nor leave such permanent scars.

Homework is the Child's Job

Kevin was in his room doing his homework. He was working on a spelling assignment for which he had to know the definitions of new words. The teacher had written the definitions on a handout, but Kevin had left it at school. Kevin's father made him look up each word in the dictionary so that he could complete the assignment. Kevin did the work under protest. He kept calling his father to come and decide which definition was the right one. Father responded in a very helpful way at first, but because he was called so often, his disposition changed. He became irritated with his son and eventually scolded and criticized him for being too lazy to do his own work.

As it turned out, Kevin's father did most of his work. He finished quickly, learned nothing, and went out to play with his friend.

It is doubtful that Kevin profited in any way from his homework. This father is "getting the education" and Kevin is proving that no one is going to *make* him learn.

Father had become Kevin's servant, for the child ordered him around and Dad obeyed his commands. He did his work for him so he could go out to play.

Homework assignments should be between the teacher and the child. The teacher could provide some sort of reinforcement to go along with homework for students like Kevin who need motivation. (Incentives like extra free time to work on favorite projects, read library books, or choose partners for a learning game could be given at school for completed homework assignments.)

It is better for parents to divorce themselves from the actual homework itself. The best way to help a child is by listening to his complaints, providing him with a good place to study, and demonstrating an interest in books and a curiosity for learning (carrying on stimulating conversations and taking him to the library).

Parents can also make deals with the child: "For every half hour you study you may earn a point. When you have earned 10 points, I will buy you the new tennis shoes you have been wanting. You could also work out an incentive program with the teacher: each day Kevin brings his homework assignments in, she will send home a baseball card. When Kevin has collected five cards, the family will go to his favorite fast food place for supper.

Parents can help by talking with their children about homework. "When do you think is the best time for you to do your work? When are you at your best? Do you understand the assignments? Can you do the work?" And if your child dawdles over his homework, "Would you like to set the timer and try to beat the clock when getting your work done? If you finish before the buzzer goes off, you can stay up 15 minutes later tonight" (or have some other privilege that the child enjoys).

When parents become more involved than this, however, by saying things like "No TV until the homework is done," there is the possibility that children will resort to lying about their assignments. Our goal is for the child to feel responsible for his work himself. As long as the parent is willing to assume responsibility for him, he will not become a self-motivated, disciplined, and responsible student.

The most important role of parents, as I see it, is to "be there:" to listen, reflect feelings, support, care, and show concern while the children are learning to assume responsibility for their own lives.

> Tom's father brought him to the library to look up information and write a report for his social studies class. He found the books Tom needed and sat him down at a table with them. Tom began complaining that he did not know how to begin. He kept whining and procrastinating, saying over and over, "I can't do this." His father tried to encourage him and help him look up the information he needed, but by this time Tom was upset and unable to accomplish anything.

> Tom's father finally took his son's notebook and wrote the report for him, while Tom wandered around the library.

Not only would Tom be turning in his father's work (which is dishonest), but his father's actions have actually increased Tom's sense of incompetency. When we do a child's work for him, we are giving him the message that he is not able to do it himself. The next time he has a difficult assignment, he will most likely con his father into doing the job for him.

Our goals are to make children confident, competent, responsible human beings. In order to do this, we need to start when they are very young by giving them jobs, assignments, and responsibilities that are appropriate for their level of development. Then we must stand back and make sure that the child does what he is expected to do. If he falters, whines, and complains, don't give in. Be patient, give him plenty of time, break the task down into manageable parts, praise small steps to the goal—but don't do the job for him.

At the time of the incident in the library, Tom's father could have moved away from the boy and busied himself with something else becoming unresponsive to his son's demands as long as he behaved in that manner. He could have insisted they leave the library and not complete the report if Tom's misbehavior continued.

To avoid such behavior in the future, the father could help prepare Tom for making reports by reviewing the necessary steps involved and by reinforcing each successful step leading to a complete paper (looking up things in an encyclopedia, etc.). Perhaps an older brother or other child Tom admires—instead of his father—could accompany Tom on his next trip to the library, showing him how to work there.

Children, like the rest of us, need to experience some bumps in the road, some falls, some failures. The sooner they become responsible for their actions, the happier and more secure they will be.

Many well-meaning parents make the mistake Tom's dad did, only to find that they are not only unappreciated, but later blamed and resented because they never helped the child become the independent and self-motivated person he needs to be.

Questions and Answers

Q. *My child says he hates school and wants to go to another school. He says that other children make fun of him, laugh at him, won't play with him, and call him bad names. I don't know how he got placed in a class with so many mean children. Why doesn't the teacher do something about it? I have talked with her and she says that she is not aware of such problems. Should I move him?*

A. I would certainly listen to what your son says, but at the same time I would remember that there must be another side to the story. Children need to learn how to get along with their peers. It could be that your son is aggravating the other children—with either his verbal or non-verbal behavior.

Perhaps you could make it your business to watch your son interacting with other children. You might invite some of his school friends to your house and listen carefully to the interaction between them. You might be able to pick up on some of the behaviors that your son is exhibiting that anger and repel others. Then you could talk with him and see if he can devise ways to help other people respond more favorably to him.

It is our responsibility as parents to help our children learn the social skills necessary to get along with others. Perhaps your son just needs some specific suggestions about things he can learn to do and say that will make others want to be with him.

If he is doing well in school otherwise, I would try to check out his social skills before I moved him.

Q. *My eight-year-old daughter and I have many fights about whether or not she needs to wear a sweater to school. Often I have to call her back after she has left for the bus stop because she forgot or failed to wear a sweater. I know she will get cold if she doesn't wear one, but she won't listen to me. Should I give up and let her get cold? I'm tired of the daily hassle.*

A. Yes, give up. Children need to learn their own body temperatures and how to take care of themselves. Let her learn the hard way. If she gets cold, she will be more likely to remember the next time. This should be her responsibility.

Q. *My children bug me to death when I get on the phone. It seems like they wait until I get involved in a conversation to act up. Invariably they scream at each other and yell for me to come. I get so aggravated that I usually allow them to ruin my telephone conversations and end up mad at them. Help!*

A. The children are trying to get your attention and they are succeeding. They have learned how to get you away from the phone—by fussing at each other and calling for your help. First of all, decide that they will no longer be successful at getting your attention. Close the door. Tune them out.

I also suggest that you work out some deals with them. The next time you are on the telephone, if they play quietly without disturbing you, they will receive a surprise—a special snack—or you will play a game with them. You might have a special set of books they could look at only while you are on the phone. Give them a choice. Either they play together nicely while you are on the phone, or they go to their rooms and stay there until they decide they can get along. In other words, reward cooperative behavior. Ignore their fussing and fighting. Refuse to get involved.

Q. *My children can find something to argue about every five minutes: whose turn it is to clear the table, which hairbrush belongs to whom, how long the other child has been in the bathroom, which TV show to watch. I get sick of being a policeman. It seems to be getting worse as they get older.*

A. There are some simple things we can do to help make life together more peaceable:

- Make charts for chores—telling who does what on which days. When they have completed their turn, they mark it off on the chart. If they forget, it's the same as if the chore hasn't been done.

- Mark all possessions that are the source of arguments with a first initial or code symbol for each child.

- Buy several timers to put in strategic places. Agree on how long a person should be on the phone or in the bathroom and set the timer.

- Encourage children to reach their own agreements over such matters as TV and toys. Let them know that if you have to step in, it will be to remove the toy, turn off the TV, or separate them until they can agree on a solution. When they realize that you will no longer take sides, they will see that it is to their advantage to work out peaceable solutions.

Q. *My son is having a terrible time trying to decide whether to drop out of college and work or go back to school. He did not do very well last year but managed to pass. We would like for him to go back, for we are afraid that he will never finish. Should we insist?*

A. A child in college needs to be self-motivated. If his heart isn't in it, he probably will not use his time wisely. Help him think through the consequences of his actions, but leave the final decision to him. He is the one who will have to live with it.

Q. *I would like to know your opinion about parents' involvement in children's homework. Do you think that parents should stay behind their children and see to it that they do their homework, or do you feel that it is not their responsibility? I feel confused because when I do get involved, I get frustrated, and when I don't help, I feel guity.*

A. Homework should be between the teacher and the student. It is almost impossible for a parent not to get subjectively involved and become uptight when the child doesn't "catch on," or when the child wants to do his work another way. It is such a temptation for the parent to step in and do the child's work, and once this has been done, the child starts relinquishing the responsibility for homework to his parent. More fights occur over homework in the home than over any other issue. Parents have a hard enough job as it is— maintaining their relationships with the children and keeping the channels of communication open—without adding the extra burden of homework.

I do think that parents should be available to help when asked—to call out spelling words and multiplication tables and to read to the child—but the major responsibility should be with the child. The teacher needs to know what the child is capable of doing and, of course, has no need to know what the parent can do. Parents should show an interest in the child's work and should make themselves available to the teacher as well as to the child, so that they can discuss the child's progress and work together to insure maximum effort.

Suggestions for the Week

1. Check some child development books out of the library. Make a list of age-appropriate behaviors for your child. Decide whether or not you think he is where you want him to be socially—able to entertain himself, take care of his own needs, pick up after himself.

2. Make a new resolution: not to do for him what he can do for himself (zip zippers, take medicine, wash his hair, collect books for school).

3. The next time your children have an argument, walk away from it. If necessary, make a phone call, go to your room, close the door, or take a walk. Say nothing.

4. When you are planning to go somewhere together in the car, discuss the trip before you leave home. Tell the children that if the noise level gets too high, you are going to pull off the road, stop, and wait for them to settle down. Do it.

5. Encourage siblings who have recurring problems (such as borrowing clothes, watching different TV programs, wanting to use the telephone at the same time) to work out compromise solutions that they can monitor and manage themselves. The bottom line—from you—might be: if plans don't work, no borrowing, TV, or telephone for anyone, until plans are back in gear.

6. Try to think of consequences you can allow your child to suffer the next time he messes up, forgets something, or is destructive. Encourage him to decide how he can make amends and then let him. Don't let him off the hook.

7. If there is someone in your child's life whom you do not care for, invite that person to your home—or to join your family for a picnic. As much as possible engage him in conversation, helping with the dishes, playing games. Let your child see him on your turf. The chances are great that much will be learned from such an occasion.

8. Talk with your child about homework. Ask if there is any way you can help him do a better job: set up a desk in a quiet spot, provide better lighting or a clock (so he can budget his time). Offer him incentives for completing his school work by a certain time (you will play a game of backgammon with him).

9. Set aside time in the week when the family reads—out loud or silently—and discusses what they have read. Use mealtime to share what you have learned from your reading.

10. Go to libraries, museums, art shows, exhibits, or boat shows with your children. Model an interest in learning, investigating, asking questions, and seeking new information.

Chapter Six

Enlist Child's Help in Rule-making

Since children come into the world not knowing how to behave, they need guidelines and rules that are at first externally placed on them by someone who is older and wiser and able to be fair, firm, and consistent. As the child matures, however, he should be allowed to be a part of the rule-making process, and shown why rules are important.

Children can sense whether we impose rules on them for their own good, or merely because we want to stay in control or are engaged in a power struggle. They have an enormous capacity for fairness and are willing to cooperate when they are allowed to take part in the decision-making process.

Too often, we adults simply assume that "We know best" and convey this to our children with "Do it because I said so." This attitude does not invite the child's cooperation. In fact, it may anger her to the point of open defiance and rebellion. If, however, we ask the child for her help and input in setting up rules, we have not only helped her practice the skills of communication and compromise, but we've also given her a real motivation to see that these rules are upheld. After all, they are hers, for she helped make them, and has an investment in seeing that they work.

Gradually the child's need for externally placed rules should become less necessary. She will be able to set up rules for herself because she understands the reasons behind them, and has developed enough self-control to live by self-imposed rules. This is our goal for children: to help them move from control that is external to that which is internal.

In our busy household, we had a rule that whenever anyone left, he would leave a note saying where he was. My youngest son kept forgetting. One day I said, "Marc, we've got to get this straight. We have got to know where you are. How can I help you remember?" (Not, "I'll tell you what to do or I'll do it for you," but "How can I help?") He said, "Well, you could spank me. I won't ever tell on you!" I said, "No. Sorry. What else could we try?" He said, "Well, I could stay in for 30 days." "30 days! Would it take a month?" "Well, maybe one day." "Okay," I said. "How about this? How about if you stay in tomorrow. Maybe that will help you remember."

Staying in was torture for Marc—he wanted to be outside with his friends. The next afternoon he got some index cards and on them he wrote "I am at Jeff's (telephone number)" "I will be at Matt's (telephone number)" "I am in the field playing ball." He made a whole filing system. After that he selected the appropriate card and put it on the counter. He used those cards for years. He came up with a creative way to solve his own problem. Children can be so much more resourceful than we are, if we just give them the chance.

Children Deserve an Explanation of the Rules

Janice was riding her shiny, blue bike over the speed bumps in the street in front of her house. Her mother came out of the house and yelled, "Janice, stop that! You're so irresponsible! I told you never to ride your bike across those bumps. Now stop!" She went back into the house and Janice kept riding across the bumps.

Later when Mom looked out the window, she saw what her daughter was doing. She opened the front door and, in an angry voice, called to Janice to come in the house "this minute."

When she entered the door, Mother slapped her hard on her back. "I had better never see you ride your bike like that again or I'll wear you out. You won't be able to sit down when I get through with you."

Later that afternoon, when Mother had gone shopping, Janice went back outside and rode her bike over the speed bumps in the street.

Mother tried to correct her child's behavior by yelling, calling her irresponsible, hitting, and threatening more severe punishment if she caught her "doing it again."

When we anger children (yell at them, call them names, and hit them) we accomplish little except to make matters worse. We seldom accomplish our goal—that of correcting their behavior. Most often, instead, we give them a reason to want to retaliate (in many cases, repeat the behavior when we are not looking). This is what happened in the case of Janice and her mother.

Mother might have handled the situation in other ways with better results. In the first place, it is very natural for an eight-year-old to want to ride over speed bumps on her bike. Mother might have accepted this as a normal part of growing up, and realized that children are going to try to do tricks and take on challenges with their bikes.

If, however, she did consider it to be dangerous, or damaging to the bike, she should have a talk with Janice. At that time she might have explained her concerns and asked for her cooperation. "The speed bumps might hurt the tires of your bike. What do you think we can do about it?" or "I'm afraid that you will wear your bike out, riding over the speed bumps. We do not have money to replace the tires. You have a choice to make. If the tires get blown out you will be without a bike until you can earn enough money to replace them, or you can stop riding over the bumps."

We cannot watch eight-year-olds all the time. Therefore, we want to make them as responsible as possible, so that they will be able to demonstrate inner control when the external controls are not present. Our goal is to try to win their cooperation.

We get the best results when we treat children with respect, and engage them in the decision-making process. "I am concerned about this problem, and I would like for us to think up some solutions together." In this way we instill the notion that within them lies the power to make good decisions. If we get them in the habit of thinking through the consequences of their actions (you may be without a bike for a while) they will begin to exercise good judgment when they are on their own because they see the wisdom in doing so—not because they might get caught or punished.

> Marilyn, fourteen, and her friend Nicole, fifteen, had decided that they would like to go bowling on Saturday morning, but they had no way to get there. Their parents had said that they were busy and could not help them out. The girls got their heads together and looked into the bus schedule. They found one that went by the bowling alley, so they agreed to ride the bus.
>
> Marilyn went to her mother and asked her if she could go on the bus to the bowling alley. Mother said, "I don't know. I don't think your father would like it. You'd better ask him first."
>
> Marilyn said, "I know what he'll say!"
>
> When she approached her dad, his answer was, "No, absolutely not!"
>
> Marilyn asked him "Why?"
>
> Dad said, "Because I said so, and I don't have to give you any reason!"
>
> Marilyn was upset with both her parents. She went upstairs and called Nicole to tell her what her father had said. After some discussion, Nicole invited Marilyn to spend Friday night with her. They agreed that they could take the bus to the bowling alley Saturday morning from Nicole's house, since *her* parents did not object. Marilyn felt bad sneaking behind her parents' back, but she thought her father deserved it, since he had not even taken the time to give her any reason for his answer.

If Mom had not wanted to make the decision by herself, she could have talked it over with Dad, so they could have agreed upon an answer. By passing the buck, she appeared to be weak and unconcerned, either of which could have made Marilyn resentful.

Both Mother and Dad discouraged Marilyn from becoming resourceful and independent. At fourteen, she is trying to learn to make decisions for herself, and she needs help and encouragement. If they had strong objections to her riding the bus, she deserved to know what they were. Because she was not treated with fairness and respect, Marilyn did what many teenagers do—retaliated with ingenuity and deceit.

Young people deserve more from us than, "Do it because I said so." Children need to learn how to think for themselves, and one of the best ways they can learn is for us to help them think through the pros and cons of their decisions.

When we exert our power and authority, and lay down orders without explanations, our children feel helpless and angry. They also learn not to trust their own ability to reason, and lose confidence in their own convictions. We say we want them to think for themselves, yet when they come up with an idea that they think is workable, we often feel irritated or inconvenienced, and without thinking it through, make a rash decision.

We owe it to our children to have good reasons for our decisions. This will teach them to have good reasons for *their* decisions. Although their plans and concerns may seem trivial to us, they are very important to them. As they grow and mature, they will have bigger decisions to make—concerning sex, drugs, education, and life goals—and they need to have the tools with which to make them.

If we try to think how we would feel if our boss talked to us in the same manner, we would think twice before we say to our teenagers, "Do it because I said so." Children need to gain confidence in their own problem-solving ability and they need as much practice as they can get while they are still young.

Help Children Set Rules for Themselves

Father dropped Annette off at the local community center dance. Annette said she would get a ride home as she had done on many previous occasions. Father agreed.

Annette arrived home after midnight. Father was angry and placed his daughter on restriction for a week, which included staying in after school and not going out the following weekend.

Annette stayed in after school all week, but on the weekend, after her parents were asleep, she climbed out of her bedroom window to catch a prearranged ride to the community center in time to enjoy the last hour of the dance. Since her "breakout" was successful, she broke curfew rules on several subsequent occasions, feeling sure that she could "get out," even if restricted.

One reason I oppose restrictions is because children tend to resist punishment by evading it or actually escaping, as Annette did. There are several alternatives that I think would have been more satisfactory and effective.

Father should have made it clear to Annette what his expectations were when he dropped her off at the dance. "What time will you be home?" or "What time do you think is reasonable?" or "I would like for you to be home by midnight." He punished her without making the expectations known in advance.

On previous occasions when Annette had arrived home on time, Father could have let her know that he appreciated it. It could be that Annette didn't think her arrival time was that important to her parents.

Annette needs to have some "in-put" on the rules that affect her. Then, if getting home on time is a recurring problem, the parents could have an understanding with her. If she gets home at the agreed-upon time, she will be free to go to the next dance. Knowing in advance the consequences of being late would give her control of her own situation. This works better for everyone involved, for it eliminates surprises, blame, and resentment.

Our goal with children is to establish the kinds of relationships within which we can state *our* needs and concerns, then allow our children the same privilege. Rules can then be mutually set and agreed upon. Having someone listen to the child's view helps her feel more inclined to cooperate.

> Mother was going to the shopping mall and she asked her sixteen-year-old son, Rich, if he would like to invite his girlfriend to go along with them. He called Carol and she said she could go.
>
> After shopping awhile, Rich asked if he and Carol could go to a movie, and Mother said it was all right with her. They agreed to call her when the movie was over to come get them.
>
> When she got home, Mother had several phone calls, so she was afraid that she might have missed their call. She called Carol's home to see if they had called there. Her dad answered, and when he found out who it was, said angrily that they had not called and that, furthermore, Carol should have been home an hour ago. Mother said she would go to the mall right away and get them.
>
> When she arrived there, Rich was alone, waiting. Carol's father had

come and taken her home. Rich said that her father was furious and cursed at both of them.

When Rich got home, he called Carol's house and spoke to her father, apologizing for not having Carol home on time. Her father, still angry, said, "Don't try to make excuses, young man. Don't bother to call her again, for Carol cannot talk to you, and you are not welcome in our house." He slammed the phone in Rich's ear.

If Carol had been told when to come home, she should have told Rich and his mother. If she had not, her father had no right to be angry. If her tardiness was intentional, her parents need to make their rules more clear and be certain that she understands the consequences ahead of time. "If you are home by 4:00, you may go with Rich the next time he invites you," or "When you come home on time, then you are free to talk on the phone that evening for a half hour."

For a sixteen-year-old to apologize to his girlfriend's father takes a lot of courage. When the father fails to accept the apology, he appears less mature than the boy. It also makes it highly unlikely that the boy will be so ready in the future to accept the responsibility for his own mistakes.

When teenagers have parents who are as strict, rigid, and unkind as Carol's father, the children often devise ways to break the rules, become devious, avoid telling their parents what's going on, and look for ways to get out of the house and beat the system. Parents who overreact, who say "no" without a reason, who pull the rug out with no warning ("You can just forget your date tonight"), who inflict inconsistent punishments and unreasonable restrictions ("You can't talk to your boyfriend for a week") are asking for trouble.

I have found that when children are made to feel this powerless and helpless, they often become bitter, retaliatory, and sneaky, and eventually become defiant, disrespectful, and callous.

All people make mistakes and need help. Teenagers are people too. They deserve to be treated with fairness, kindness, and dignity. As they grow and mature, we should strive to grow alongside them—in our ability to communicate and live together in mutual respect, honesty, and love.

Negotiate Rules Calmly

The family had a rule that the children could not watch TV if there were any clothes that needed to be folded and put away. When the clothes were dry, Mother put them in a chair in the den, so it was obvious to the children when there was work to do.

Dad was the first to arrive home from work, and when he entered the den, he found the clothes piled high in the chair and the three children watching a television program.

Angry, he walked to the TV, turned it off, and demanded that the children start folding clothes. He grumbled that they couldn't do the simplest things on their own initiative and that he was sick and tired of that chair being the repository for unfolded clothes.

Enlist Child's
Help in
Rule-making

The children began arguing among themselves. "I folded the last load." "No, you didn't, you scab, I did. You only folded two things. I did all the rest." "You just pretended to fold them, what you actually did was wad them up and deliberately wrinkle the shirt I was planning to wear to school."

The argument escalated in volume until finally their father had had all he could take. He banished them to their rooms. There the verbal battle continued, with much loud and vicious talk.

Downstairs, Dad became furious because he could still hear the arguments. He finally marched upstairs with a heavier-than-normal tread, and threatened to restrict them all until they were thirty. He ordered them to start being "sweet to each other." He told the sixteen-year-old that he could just forget ever driving the family car if he couldn't remember a simple thing like folding clothes. He told the girls that they wouldn't be doing any swimming this summer if they didn't "toe the straight and narrow."

Seething inside, Dad returned downstairs and folded the clothes himself, so he would have a place to sit and read the newspaper. The children joined forces against the common enemy and agreed that parents were unfair, mean, and crazy. When dinner was ready, the children were called downstairs, and the family ate in strained silence.

Scenes such as this are typical in many families. Although rules like "no TV until the clothes are folded" are basically a good idea, if they don't work they should be renegotiated or abolished.

Perhaps the family could talk together to come up with other deals about the clothes. It might be better if a job were given to each child, instead of a joint assignment made to all three. Then there would be no competition to see who could get out of work. The children might make a chart to hang on the refrigerator door. Each would have a day when it was his turn to fold the clothes. When his job was done, he could check it off, and the next child would know it is his turn. When left on their own to devise impartial divisions of labor, children can invent ingenius ways to be fair and still get the job done.

In this case, the children succeeded in getting out of the work—their dad did it for them. No wonder he was resentful. He allowed himself to take on the responsibility of the clothes and the children were happy to let him.

Threatening to restrict the children until they reach the age of thirty, telling the son that he would never drive the car, and telling the girls that they wouldn't swim this summer did no good. When parents resort to idle threats and bluffing, children lose respect and learn not to take them seriously. Since it is the children's respect that parents want and need, they should be careful not to resort to saying things that jeopardize the relationship.

Mother was able to leave work earlier than usual and decided to hurry home and take Beth to the beach. She thought that her daughter would be excited. When she opened the front door and called to her, she heard some scrambling in the den. Beth did not answer her. Mother had a funny feeling in her stomach as she headed toward the den.

Beth met her at the door. On the sofa behind Beth, she saw Dean, the boy next door, looking very embarrassed and scared.

Mother's heart sank. She had been leaving Beth alone all summer, with the clear understanding that she was not to let anyone in the house while Mother was gone. She had called Beth several times a day to check on her and had never suspected that she was not obeying her.

Mother flew into a rage. She ordered Dean to leave the house and NEVER come there again. The boy, saying nothing, hurried out the door.

Then she started in on Beth, "Here I thought I could trust you. Is this what you've been doing all summer? The minute my back is turned, you take advantage of me. What do you think you're doing? Don't you know the neighbors are probably talking? Are you a tramp? I'll never be able to trust you now; I'm going to send you to spend the rest of the summer with Aunt Eloise. Then you can't get into trouble with Dean. You are never to lay eyes on him again. Is that clear?!"

Mother felt like a screaming maniac. She went into her bedroom, slammed the door, and locked it. Beth was stunned. She started crying and knocking on her mother's door. "Please let me explain, Mom. This is the first time Dean has come over here. Please don't send me to Aunt Eloise's. I can't stand it. I won't go. You can trust me. Please talk to me."

Mother wouldn't answer. She called Aunt Eloise and asked if she could bring Beth over. She told Beth to pack her clothes. The child refused, so Mother packed for her. That night, she drove Beth to Aunt Eloise's without a word.

Many parents face traumatic circumstances like these at one time or another. Children are naturally going to disobey and disappoint us at times. We have a tendency to exaggerate circumstances and blow them out of proportion. We often say hurtful things we don't mean and instead of solving the problems that exist, we create additional ones.

The way we face disappointments is very important, for when the going gets rough, children resort to handling their problems the way they have been taught—by example.

It is always a good idea to cool down before issuing ultimatums. It might have been wise for Mother to have told Beth that she needed time alone to think. Of course it is acceptable to express feelings of hurt and disappointment, but it is better to wait until you have had time to get some perspective before you make decisions which involve the future.

In this case, perhaps Mother had expected too much of Beth—to think that she would be content to stay at home alone all day. This would have been a good time to have a meaningful dialogue concerning the rules, needs, and feelings of the young adolescent. When Mother was feeling more rational, she might have asked Beth what she thought was fair. Together they could have come up with some compromises that both could accept and live with. Maybe Beth could spend her days at Aunt Eloise's or at a day camp, so that she could have both something to do and adult supervision.

It is unrealistic to tell a child that she cannot see the boy next door ever again. There is no way that Mother can enforce such a rule. She cannot become her child's bodyguard. Instead, it would be better to tell Beth honestly what she is afraid of, so that they can talk together about the real issues.

Our best hope is to teach and train children to make wise decisions on their own behalf, so that when temptation comes, they have the wisdom and judgment they need. We never want our children to think we have given up on them. Then they will be tempted to give up on themselves. When they make unwise decisions, we need to step in and talk with them as rationally as possible, to help them learn from their small mistakes before they have to learn a harder way—by making bigger mistakes that could drastically affect their futures.

Jessica and her mother were engaged in a heated argument over what time the daughter should come home after her date. Mother felt that 11:00 was reasonable, but Jessica reported that "Everybody stays out until midnight."

Both of them began arguing—cursing and yelling. Finally Jessica announced that she was going to stay out until midnight, no matter what her mother said, and she stormed out of the room.

Mother shrugged her shoulders. "What's the use?" she muttered to herself.

That night Jessica stayed out until 12:30. She had gotten away with cursing and yelling, and had won the power struggle with her mother. The chances are great that she will show little regard for her mother's wishes in the future.

This is a sad state of affairs: sad for Mother not to have earned more regard from her daughter, and sad for the child that she has not been taught respect for authority.

Parents need to stay in the driver's seat as long as their children are dependent on them: physically, emotionally, or financially. This does not mean that they should lay down ultimatums, for these can backfire and cause children to rebel.

Nevertheless, communication does not have to break down to this low level. Both mother and daughter need help. Perhaps a third party could be more objective and could help them learn appropriate, respectful, and healthy ways to communicate.

Good communication works both ways. A seventeen-year-old should be able to state her case—telling what she wants and why she thinks it is fair. Mother also needs to be able to communicate her feelings rationally. Perhaps a compromise could be made. However, this needs to be worked out before Jessica leaves the house. She needs to respect her mother enough to obey her and her mother needs to respect her enough to be able to listen objectively to her feelings.

Perhaps some deals could be made. "When you have come home on time for three nights straight, then we will allow you to stay out fifteen minutes later the next night." "When you have come home on time for five nights, then we'll go shopping for new shoes."

Life with teenagers is a constant battle if every issue becomes a power struggle. It can be challenging and fun when all people concerned feel that they have an equal chance to be heard, their feelings and concerns are taken seriously, and compromises are negotiated to the mutual satisfaction of all.

Help Children Outgrow Their Need For External Rules

One night my son Marc got a phone call and he said to me, still on the phone, "Mom, can I go to a basketball game tonight?" I said, "Well, Marc, I don't know. I think that's up to you to decide. You know how much work you have to do." "Yeah, I can go," he said to the person on the other end, and hung up. He left the room, and I didn't say anything to him. He came back downstairs in about five minutes and dialed his friend on the phone and said, "I can't go to the game. No, she didn't say I couldn't. It's just that I have too much work to do." And he hung up. He turned to me and grinned. And I grinned.

I thought, now if I had said, "You can't go, you have too much work to do," then he'd have been mad at me all night. This way I wasn't in there at all: he's making the decisions, he doesn't have anybody to be mad at. If I had told him he couldn't go because he needed to stay home and do his homework, he might have stayed home begrudgingly and done a halfway job on his homework.

It is important that we help children become responsible for their own decisions. We need to help them learn to think ahead of the consequences of their actions ("How will I feel tomorrow if I don't have my homework done?") and make wise choices based on the future. Of course this will involve making mistakes. We have to learn how it feels to eat too much candy by eating too much candy. Then we learn to be more careful.

Children need to learn to consider their alternatives. "I can sit up too late and be tired tomorrow, or I can go to bed on time and be rested." If parents are telling their children what to do all the time the children will never get the chance to explore their own options.

I have often thought that we always have alternatives, and this is what we want to teach children. Even if you are a prisoner of war and tied in a chair, you still have alternatives: you can look up or down, or close your eyes. You can pray, sing, hum, cry, meditate, or think. You always have alternatives. Teach your child that he has alternatives and help him learn that no matter what obstacle is placed in front of him, he can choose to make it a stumbling block or a stepping stone. The choice is his.

Questions and Answers

Q. *I have a friend with a child the same age as mine. We like to take our children places together and to visit in each other's homes. However, I feel that her son is constantly taking advantage of our daughter. Whenever they are at our house, he wants whatever she is playing with, and whenever we are in their home, he says she can't have his toys. His mother never intervenes. Should I say something to the mother, to the child, or should I leave them alone?*

A. I think it would be fine for you to talk privately with your friend's child. Make some deals with him. Tell him that if he will let your daughter play with his toys at his house, you will let him play with her toys when he comes to visit. Sometimes it works better when these deals are made in private and no one else is involved.

Q. *Now that our daughter is a teenager, my husband and I seem to be in disagreement more than ever. He feels that we need to keep tabs on her more than I do. He quizzes her about everything she does, and I can tell that it really bugs her. I feel that she needs her privacy, and if she wants to tell us what she is doing, she will volunteer the information. What do you think? She is seventeen.*

A. I do feel that we can turn our children off by being too inquisitive. Since they spend their teenage years trying to find themselves and establish their own identity, they have a strong need for independence and respect. We do much better to let them know that we are there if they need us, and to give them the space they need to figure out things for themselves as they try to get it all together.

Q. *Our son is seventeen and very interested in a girl. He has a part-time job, but is still dependent on us for financial support. We help him out in many ways, including letting him borrow our car for dates. Do you think we* *still have a right to expect him to obey our rules, stick by a curfew, and help out around the house, or is he too old for such things?*

A. You certainly do have the right (and obligation) to help him become a responsible adult. As long as he lives in your house and is in any way dependent on you, I feel he owes it to you to consider your wishes, to cooperate, help you, and let you know he'll be in at a reasonable hour. I would suggest that you discuss such matters with him and agree ahead of time on what is fair and reasonable. Then make it clear that you expect him to live up to his end of the bargain.

Q. *When do you think children are too old for curfews? Our daughter has finished one year of college, and this summer she is complaining about our rules. She says that she got along fine all year away from home with no one checking up on her. She resents our interference and says that she doesn't want to be treated like a baby. What is your feeling about all of this?*

A. I think children should be accountable to their parents as long as their parents are supporting them financially. Of course, agreements and arrangements should be negotiated and made as peaceably as possible. It should not be necessary to lay down rules—unless the child is unable to control herself and needs help in structuring her life.

Children should be reasonable, responsible, respectful of their parents' needs, and, most of all, trustworthy. In other words, they should say where they are going and when they will be home. Then they should be expected to live up to their word.

Suggestions for the Week

1. Make a list of all the rules that exist at your house—and who is expected to abide by them (leaving notes, asking to be excused from the table, watching only a certain number of hours of TV a day, calling if you are going to be late getting home.)

2. Discuss these rules with your family.

3. Ask which rules they think are fair and which are unfair. Ask if they think some are unnecessary and should be eliminated or changed. Which ones do they feel they have outgrown?

4. Solicit suggestions for changing some of the rules that are not being followed or that are resented.

5. Implement changes. Set a time limit for trying the new rules.

6. After a week or two (whatever has been agreed upon), call the family together again. Discuss the new arrangements.

7. Make sure that children of different ages have different sets of rules (different bedtimes, amounts of freedom, etc.). Emphasize the fact that as children exhibit more responsibility and less need for rules, they will be given more freedom.

8. Encourage children to set rules for themselves. (If you want to lose weight, how many calories do you think you should try to limit yourself to? What can you cut out? How much weight is it realistic to try to lose in a month? How can I help you? If your book report is due in two weeks, how many pages could you read a day to have it read in time? If you want to save enough money for a new tape recorder, how many lawns would you have to mow each week in order to have it by July 4?)

9. Expose your child to role models who have had to sacrifice for their achievements. Engage these people in conversations concerning their short-term and long-term goals, and the effort that is necessary to reach them. (If you want to make the basketball team, you will have to practice shooting baskets, running, and maybe working out this summer to get yourself in shape for the team. If you think you'd like to be a nurse someday, perhaps it would be a good idea to volunteer for work in the hospital to see how you like being around sick people. If you think you would like to be a singer, perhaps you should set aside an hour a day to listen to recordings and vocalize and learn new music.)

10. Choose a new skill you would like to acquire yourself. Tell your family about it. Set a course of action, and get started. Ask for their support and encouragement.

Chapter Seven

Encourage Individuality

The seventh principle, which is very important, is to treat your child as an individual and encourage him to be unique. So many parents ask "How can two children born to the same parents, who live in the same home, turn out to be so different?" The answer is simple: they are *trying* to be different; they have a need to be different. None of us wants to be a carbon copy of another person.

It is a common mistake of parents and teachers to say, "Why can't you be like your sister? She makes good grades, is responsible, dependable, pretty..." This sends a child in the opposite direction. If his sister is all those good things, and he needs to be different (which he does) what will he be? Irresponsible? Unreliable? A poor student? Sometimes we give a child no choice but to develop all the negative traits—because he has this need to be different.

There is a way to combat this problem: encourage differentness. Find an area of expertise for each child. Do not compare children or force them to compete for your love and attention.

Sibling Rivalry is Natural

Daddy was preparing formula for the two-month-old when he noticed an empty baby bottle by the sink. He realized that his four-year-old son Jeremy had drunk the orange juice from his sister's bottle and left it on the counter.

Daddy got hysterical and started screaming at his son. "What's wrong with you? Are you a baby? I don't know what to do with you. Do you want me to put diapers on you?"

He smacked his bottom and told him to get out of his sight.

Jeremy left the room in tears. He went upstairs and started pulling toys out of his toy box. When Daddy came up later, he found him asleep, lying on the floor in the middle of his toys.

Jeremy's interest in his sister's baby bottle is natural. All children at times feel resentful of their younger siblings because they have to share their parents' time and attention.

Children have different ways of showing their jealousy. Some of them show it in obvious ways—wanting to drink out of baby bottles, be rocked, suck their thumbs, or talk baby talk.

Other children are more subtle. They find new ways to misbehave and call attention to themselves. They wet their beds, act bratty in public, fight with other children, become disobedient or destructive.

Parents and teachers need to be especially sensitive to the older child when a new baby appears on the scene. I think it is a mistake to send the older child away—either to spend time away from home, or to be alone in another part of the house. One of his biggest fears is that of being replaced, and we need to make every effort to help him feel that such is not the case.

An older child will probably need to regress for a while and pretend that he is a baby again. It will not hurt to rock him, let him drink out of a bottle, or talk baby talk for a while until he can get it out of his system. It is helpful to remember that when a need is met, it is outgrown. When the child has had enough babying, he will let you know, and the need for it will disappear. Most likely the child will then take pride in being the older sister or brother. Some children like to help feed the baby or give her a bottle. Some like to entertain her or carry the diaper bag.

It is wise to give the oldest child special privileges and help him see that his place has very distinct benefits. It also helps to let him know that the younger child will look up to him someday and copy the things she sees him do. This role of teacher is especially valuable to older children and benefits them in many ways.

It is too much to expect children to be thrilled with the intrusion of a sibling. (How would I feel if my husband announced to me one day that he was bringing another wife home to live with us? Even though he might try to reassure me that I would still be important, I would have serious misgivings!) Children learn to exhibit the appropriate "love the baby" behavior because it is expected and reinforced. However, we need to look beneath the surface now and then. Hopefully siblings can learn to love and appreciate each other as they grow, each feeling unique and secure with his own distinct place in the family.

When Father first entered the waiting room, he went to the window and told the nurse that he had just called about the baby's symptoms. The nurse said that the doctor would see him in a few minutes, and asked him to be seated in the waiting room. When he sat down, he started rocking the baby and told three-year-old Amy to play with the toys. She went over and pushed a truck, then stopped and looked at her father, who was still rocking and talking to the baby. Amy went over and started to hug Jay, her little brother. Father told her to stop because she might hurt the baby, who was very sick.

Amy looked disappointed and started to pout. Father told her to "act like a big girl" and go and play. She went back over to the truck and kicked it. It hit the wall with a thud. Jay started to cry. Father got up, pulled Amy over to one of the chairs, and told her to sit down and stop being so bad. He told her that the baby could get sicker if she cried too much. Amy sat quietly for awhile.

In a few minutes, Amy said her tummy hurt. Father, still patting the baby, told her not to let the doctor hear her because she might get a shot.

The nurse finally called them into the doctor's office.

Amy learned that she can't go near her baby brother and hug him when he's sick. She also learned that if she said *she* was sick, her father wouldn't be as concerned as when the baby was sick. Father taught her that if she was sick the doctor would probably give her a shot.

Although it is difficult not to show favoritism when a child is ill, we need to be careful to look out for the needs of the other children.

Father might have talked with Amy on the way to the doctor's office and explained how worried he was about the baby. He could have asked her ahead of time to please try to play quietly while they waited, and when they had gotten the baby taken care of, they could go back home and spend time reading or playing a game together.

He might have let her feel more a part of things when she wanted to soothe the baby, by letting her pull up a chair and pat his arm.

Surely he made more trouble by letting Amy know that he wasn't concerned about her sick tummy, and that if she wasn't quiet, the doctor would have to hurt her with a shot.

It was Jimmy's first day of school. His parents had prepared him for the big event by buying him new clothes, shoes, lunchbox, pencils, and pencil case. He had been taken to see his new school and to meet his teacher. They had gotten up early that morning and taken movies of each event: getting dressed, eating breakfast, walking out the door, boarding the school bus.

Mother cried a little as the bus rounded the corner. She and Daddy walked slowly to the house, talking about how cute Jimmy was and how fast he had grown up.

When they got back to the house, Mother went upstairs to wake his younger brother Billy. He was not in his room. She called but got no answer. She looked around for him and asked Daddy to help. Daddy looked in the garage and there he found Billy sitting on the floor in the midst of tires, pedals, fenders, and bicycle parts. He had taken his bike apart and was pounding on the fenders with a hammer.

Daddy called to Mother, "Here he is, Lillian—making a mess in the garage." To Billy, he said angrily, "What do you think you're doing—ruining your bicycle? Boy, why do you have to take everything apart? Why look at Jimmy's. It's all shiny and clean. Why can't you be like him? He takes good care of his things—and you ruin everything you can get your hands on. You'll never be ready for school. I don't know what they are going to do with you when they get you. They won't know what hit them. Get in here. Go to your room and stay there until I say you can come out."

Daddy went back in the house to eat breakfast. Billy got up slowly. As he walked by Jimmy's bike, he kicked it with his foot and knocked it off its kickstand.

Billy had watched Jimmy get much attention during the past several days, and his jealousy got the best of him. This is not at all unusual. Parents need to be aware of these feelings between children and take care not to add to the problems that naturally exist.

If treated carefully, sibling rivalry (the competition of brothers and sisters for the love and attention of their parents) is mild and can be outgrown. If it is mishandled or aggravated, it can spill over into peer competition for friends, grades and sports.

Psychiatrists say that 25 percent of us carry sibling rivalry into our adulthood, like excess baggage. It surfaces as competition for the limelight, jealousy of our colleagues, and an inability to share those we love with others.

The messages we give our children come back to us loud and clear. If one child is viewed as "perfect" the other child may try to excel in "imperfection."

Growing up with siblings can be beneficial. With careful handling, brothers and sisters can learn to depend on each other, share with each other, and help one another. Ideally they can develop a strong sense of loyalty and cooperation which will be a valuable asset as they grow older.

Putting Siblings in Charge of Other Siblings Spells Trouble

Paul, nine, was washing his father's car. His little sister Nina, six, came out of the garage and stood watching him.

Paul looked at her and said, "Nina, go put some shoes on." Nina didn't answer, but instead started splashing in the water with her feet.

"Get in the house, Nina. You're not getting me in trouble again." Nina started jumping in the water.

Paul threw the rag down and went in the house. Nina walked to a dry part of the driveway and sat down.

When Paul came back, Mother was with him.

"She had her feet in the water and she won't put her shoes on," Paul said.

Nina jumped up. "I did not."

"You did too."

"Did not."

"Did too!"

"I did not!" Nina screamed.

Paul punched her in the nose.

His mother swatted Paul's backside, saying, "I'll be the one to discipline Nina. Go to your rooms, both of you."

Mother finished hosing off the car. When their father came home, he put both children on restriction for a week.

In this case, Paul got in trouble because he was trying to look out for his sister. Evidently he had been put in charge of her before and felt that he would be held accountable for her again. Nina learned that she could get her brother in trouble by lying and making him mad enough to hit her. Probably she has used this tactic before and will use it again.

Although it is a temptation for parents to put older children in charge of younger ones, the problems that often result can be damaging. In the first place, such an arrangement does not endear siblings to each other. The younger one usually resents being bossed around, and the older feels burdened by the responsibility for another person. Each sibling is forced to learn negative devices—such as trickery, bribery, tattling, bossing, threatening, and aggravating—to cope with such an arrangement, which may carry over into other relationships, both present and future.

If something should happen to the younger child, the older sibling could be scarred for life with the guilt and blame he might feel. I know of three cases where older children have felt responsible for tragedies that happened to their younger siblings when they had been left in charge. One neglected to watch his little brother closely enough and the child fell into the backyard pool and drowned. Another left the house for a few minutes to talk to friends and her little sister fell and later died from a concussion. A third was left in charge when two younger brothers were horsing around, shooting paper clips at each other. One of the children lost the sight in one eye as a result of a misguided clip.

It is difficult enough for adults to forgive themselves for their children's accidents, but it is almost impossible for siblings not to develop severe emotional problems when they feel such a tragedy was their fault.

The car-washing incident could have been avoided if six-year-old Nina had been put in charge of her own bare feet and shoes. There was no need for Paul to become involved in such an unimportant matter.

Parents often bemoan the fact that their children fight all the time. It is my hunch that we build sibling rivalry and jealousy when we put children in charge of children. We would get better results if we help each child to feel responsible for himself as early as possible.

First, it will develop self-control and responsibility, and second, it will help brothers and sisters grow up together without added resentment and jealousy. In addition, there will be more room for the cultivation of positive feelings for each other, such as genuine love, concern, and caring, which all parents want for their children, both now and in the years to come.

> Mother was working in the flower bed and four-year-old Ed was in the backyard with her. He kept pestering her to stop working and play with him. Mother was busy and didn't have time to stop. Margaret, seven, was upstairs in her room playing alone. Ed complained that he didn't have anything to do. Mother told him to go in and play with Margaret.
>
> In a few minutes he came back and told her that Margaret wouldn't let him come in her room. This made Mother angry, so she went in the house and called Margaret, "Come here this minute!"
>
> When her daughter came downstairs, Mother said, "Why wouldn't you let Ed come in your room and play with you?" Margaret said that she was reading and didn't want to play with him. "Well, I don't care what you want, young lady. You come outdoors where we are and play with Ed. He wants some company."
>
> Reluctantly, Margaret came outside and started swinging. Immediately Ed wanted her swing. He tried to push her off the seat. She hollered for help, but Mother told her to get off the swing and let Ed have a turn. After all, she was the oldest and should set a good example for her little brother.
>
> Mother went in to start dinner while Margaret was swinging Ed. In a few minutes, she heard screaming from the backyard. She looked out the window and found them engaged in a first-class physical battle. Furious, she ran out into the yard and grabbed both the children. She spanked them and sent them to their rooms without dinner.

It is natural for a child of four to want his mother to stop what she is doing to play with him, and it is understandable that she doesn't always have the time to do so. The problem should be worked out between them, however, without dragging in another child to solve it.

We run the risk of making our children dislike each other when we ask one child to stop what he is doing to look out for a younger sibling who is already in a grumpy and unpleasant mood. The results are most often unsatisfactory, and, in fact, the final outcome is actually worse than the initial problem.

Brothers and sisters "happen" into the same family—not by choice—and they have no reason to like the idea or love and be glad for the existence of the other.

It is the job of parents to teach children to love and care for one another. Many parents inadvertently do the opposite by actually intensifying hostility and jealousy between brothers and sisters.

Our first responsibility is to help each child feel good about himself. Hopefully he will then have the desire, the energy, and the time to see his brother or sister not as a competitor but as a companion, and together they can cultivate the closeness, caring, and concern that we would like our children to have for one another.

Building Skills and Competence Encourages Individuality

Two-year-old Carol was sitting in the middle of the floor playing with her blocks, while Mom and Daddy were watching. She was enthusiastically building castles and taking great pleasure in knocking them down. Mom and Dad were attentively responding to Carol's "look's" with "Oh's" and claps and laughing smiles. Their undivided attention spurred her on to making bigger castles that came down with louder crashes.

John, eleven, entered the living room, proudly displaying the wooden plane he had been working on since early afternoon. He walked over to show his prize to his father. Dad, barely looking away from Carol, said, "Did you put away my tools? Probably not. You know what I told you about scattering my tools from here to creation."

John told his dad he hadn't finished with them yet, and turned to his mom. "See, Mom! And I'm going to paint a door here and windows, and see, I made a propeller with cardboard and rubber bands."

Mom looked and responded, "Shouldn't you have used popsicle sticks instead?"

"It's just for looks," John said quietly. "It's not supposed to fly."

John left the room, the plane dangling by his side.

Later, re-entering the room with new enthusiasm, John held up his newly painted plane and exclaimed, "I'm gonna call it the Tilantic." He glanced at his parents for some sign of approval.

Not looking up, his mom responded, "Don't you mean Titanic? That's a ship, not a plane. Why don't you call it the Spirit of St. Louis instead?"

"Yeah," said John, trying to sound excited. "That's a good name. Better than my dumb old name." Turning, he walked dejectedly out of the room.

John failed to put Dad's tools away that night.

The boy's attempt to explore his creative talents was transformed into the task of making something that would get his parents' approval. John's confidence in his decision-making abilities was stifled by the unasked-for suggestions of his mom, and the "I'll bet you didn't do what I asked" attitude of his dad. As a result he had little incentive to obey his father's wishes and put away the tools.

It was obvious to John that his parents were not too enthusiastic about his creative attempts. His father was more interested in being sure that his tools were in their proper place. John might well conclude that his sister's activities were more important to his parents than his were.

Both parents could have responded positively to John's efforts, by praising his project rather than emphasizing his incompetence. Instead of reminding John of past negligence, Dad could have gently given him a positive cue, such as, "I left the tool room open for you when you're finished."

By correcting John and giving unsolicited advice, Mother was discouraging him from feeling adequate. Even Carol could have been encouraged to give attention to her brother, "Look, Carol, at the plane John made."

We unconsciously contribute to sibling rivalry and jealousy when we give undue attention to one child and neglect to encourage the other for positive behavior and obvious effort.

> Father was keeping his eye on seven-year-old Jerry while trying to get some work done in the garage. Mr. Moore, the next door neighbor, came over with his tools to help with some woodworking.
>
> Father handed Jerry a soccer ball and told him to go play. Then he began to work with Mr. Moore.
>
> Jerry bounced the ball half-heartedly in the front yard for a few minutes, but seeing no other children around and attracted by the buzz of motors, he wandered over to the garage.
>
> "Get out of here," Father snapped, without turning around. Jerry moved a few paces away. As more wood chips flew through the air and the machinery noises became more inviting, Jerry once again ventured closer.
>
> "Get out or I'll bust your butt," Father yelled again.
>
> "I only want to watch," said Jerry.
>
> "You are too dumb to understand what we are doing here, and anyway, I told you to get out. Now get!"
>
> Jerry changed his tactics and walked around to the garage window, where he stood watching the two men work. Suddenly, he heard an

exclamation from his father and saw blood streaming from his hand. Jerry ran around the garage and in the open door.

When Father saw Jerry in the garage again, he picked up the nearest large piece of wood and started after him. "Didn't I tell you to get out of here?" he bellowed. Jerry ran.

A few days later, some boys sneaked into Mr. Moore's garage and took some of his woodworking tools. A power drill was later found, broken, in the street. Under duress, Jerry admitted taking the tools and was severely punished.

Children are naturally curious and want to be included in their parents' work. In this case, what Father and his neighbor were doing was especially interesting to Jerry. Since he had no one to play with, and Mother was gone, his curiosity was understandable.

By sending Jerry away, Father probably made him feel that he was unimportant and too small to understand or be helpful. Feeling "in the way" is not a good way to feel. It makes children lose their self-confidence, and then they often become a nuisance.

It would have helped if Father had involved Jerry in the woodworking. This was an excellent opportunity to teach him a few skills and to make him aware of safety rules. He could have given him some wood of his own, and a knife with which to carve—or he might have taken this chance to teach him how to use some of the simpler tools and help the child develop a real interest in woodworking. (A busy child doesn't cause trouble like a bored child does.)

Because he was treated with anger, Jerry retaliated by sneaking into Mr. Moore's garage and taking his tools. This incident could have been prevented if Father had made Jerry feel that he was important enough to have been included in the men's work.

Barbara, who was in the eighth grade, was upset about one of the policies at the junior high school. She wrote a letter to the school newspaper and, very proud of her accomplishment, showed it to her mother.

When Mother read the letter, she saw some misspelled words and grammatical errors. She corrected them and then proceeded to reword some of the sentences. When she gave it back to Barbara, she could tell that her daughter was disappointed. Mother said, "I just fixed it up

and changed some of the sentences so they would sound better."
Barbara copied over the changed version of the letter and turned it in
to the school newspaper. Nothing else was said and Mother forgot
about the letter.

Several weeks later, while vacuuming Barbara's room, she saw the
school newspaper lying on her desk. She picked it up and saw
Barbara's letter on the front page. When her daughter came home, she
said to her, "I saw your letter in the school newspaper. Why didn't you
show it to me?"

Barbara responded without enthusiasm, "It wasn't *my* letter. It was
yours."

Mother, by changing Barbara's work, had caused Barbara to lose her
enthusiasm and confidence. If Mother had been more supportive of Barbara's
creative efforts, she could have prevented this. When children take the initiative
to tackle a creative venture, they should be encouraged as much as possible.
When we step in to correct, judge, and alter their efforts, we run the risk of
stifling their creative impulses—to the point where they may become satisfied
with complacency and mediocrity.

Mother and Father and their three children were eating dinner in a
restaurant. When the waiter announced the dessert selections, everyone
asked for pumpkin pie except Nelwyn, four, who requested a brownie.

Mother ignored her daughter's request and said, "Good. We'll all have
pumpkin pie. That's a nice dessert."

Nelwyn was very unhappy and started whining. Other diners began to
pay attention to the child as she became louder. Embarrassed, Mother
kept asking Nelwyn to "please be quiet."

Finally, out of desperation, she slapped Nelwyn's hand and told her
that she would have to eat pumpkin pie and like it.

When the pie came, Nelwyn pushed it away and refused to eat. Mother
begged her to at least taste it, but Nelwyn was not interested. The pie
was left untouched.

In the first place, Mother caused the scene by trying to dominate the situation
and dictate Nelwyn's choice of dessert. Many parents fall into this trap and then
become frustrated with the resulting misbehavior.

Children deserve the right to be treated as persons with likes and preferences of their own. They need to be allowed to make choices at an early age, and it is the parents' role to provide the opportunity for wise and appropriate choices.

There are many times when choices are not possible, such as at home where there are no other desserts to choose from. Then the child should be allowed to decide whether or not she wants to eat the dessert that is provided.

It is important that each child be treated in an individual manner. This validates her as a separate person, important in her own right. Nothing makes one madder than being automatically included as part of a group, or blamed for something she hasn't done.

As an adult, I still don't like it when in choir practice, the director says, "The sopranos didn't get the timing right." It makes me angry when I know I had it right. Do you know what it makes me do? Not want to sing. He lumped us all together and assumed that we all messed up. That makes me mad, and I still rebel.

When a teacher says, "You children are not paying attention," there is usually at least one child who *is* paying attention. That child thinks to himself, "Well, why should I pay attention? I'm not going to anymore. It doesn't pay to obey."

Treat each child individually, and let each one find a specialness. In a family it's so important. Each child needs to feel that she is unique. Give her something to do that's special. "You're my duster. You're my cake decorator. You're the one I can count on to help me remember my grocery list." Let each child be glad for her differentness.

Don't let all the children take piano lessons. Let one child try guitar, another ballet. Because they'll compete. And one is going to give up. If you can't be best, it's easy to quit trying. That's what happens in families: "Why can't you be like Johnny? Mary makes good grades, Sally gets her bed made." "Well, I don't want to be Johnny, or Mary, or Sally. I want to be me."

My first two children made good grades as they went through school, doing most of the "expected" things. My third child said, "I'm not going to do any of that." And we went, "Uh-oh." What he wanted to do was play drums. We let him get a drum set, and told him he could practice in the attic for the summer. He took drum lessons, and actually became quite good. By fall we let him bring the

drums in the house. We made two rules: not to play if anyone's asleep, and to stop if anyone asked him to. He was thrilled. (Just knowing that he would stop if we asked him to made all of us free to enjoy his music.)

The other two children thought he was special, because he could play those drums. They couldn't play. They brought their friends in to see him. This gave him a specialness. Then he didn't need to get bad grades to be different. After that he didn't have as much need to be different. So it was okay for him to do many of the things that the other children did. As a matter of fact, he followed in their footsteps in many ways.

Children have energy to burn and they reach out in all directions. If we are wise, we will expose them to as many areas of interest as possible, and then allow them to choose the ones most suitable for them. It is only through trial and error that they are able to find out where their natural talents and inclinations lie. Every child can excel in something: swimming, tennis, ping pong, music, gymnastics, crocheting, cooking, camping, embroidering, basketball, or painting. Children should be encouraged to compete against themselves—to improve their skills week by week—not to do better than someone else. It works best when they excel in areas that are different from those chosen by their siblings. This eliminates competition and discouragement.

When children find their niche, their attention span is incredible. I remember when my sons started shooting baskets. They would forget to eat! They would stay outdoors by the hour—many times they would forget to wear a sweater and come in just purple, having stayed through lunch, for five hours, shooting baskets, over and over.

You've seen a child when he learns to tie his shoes—the first thing he does is untie them and tie them again. That sweet smell of success!

We want to give that to children.

We rob the child of self-respect when we do for him what he can do for himself. Children want to be competent, confident, and independent. The ones who have lots of skills, who can take care of themselves, will not be as likely to get in trouble. They won't have as much need to fall in with their peers, act just like the peers, and do everything the peers are doing. They'll be too busy doing other things.

We will be helping our children become competent when we:

- Encourage their efforts.
- Support their interests.
- Offer broad exposure and many options.
- Provide opportunities for them to develop new skills.

We should not try to:

- Do their work for them.
- Make excuses for them.
- Pressure, compare, criticize, or humiliate them.
- Undermine their efforts.
- Show disappointment it they don't enjoy the same things we enjoy.

We need to remember that each child possesses a drive for mastery. We should try to see beyond the smoke screen of grumpiness and indifference and know that they will like themselves better when they feel good about what they can master. Increasing self-reliance builds self-esteem. If we encourage children to develop skills early in life, we are giving them the tools needed to withstand some of the pressures that come with adolescence and we will help them be able to say one day, "I know who I am and trust my capacity to handle my life responsibly."

Questions and Answers

Q. *Our two children are constantly comparing our love for them. Each insists that we love the other the most, and challenges many of our decisions with, "How come you let her and you won't let me?" Do all families have to deal with this?*

A. Some sibling rivalry is inevitable. However, we can minimize the jealousy if we are careful to treat each child as an individual. We should encourage their "differences" and build on their strengths. It is best if they can excel in different areas. Help each to find a "specialty" (singing, tennis, skating, crocheting). Try to spend time with each alone.

Children need to feel good about themselves, and constant comparison breeds jealousy and insecurity.

Q. *My problem is with our son Josh (three) and our dog Fritz, who is nine-years-old. Of course, we had Fritz long before Josh was born, so we did not anticipate any problems. We have been especially careful to treat Fritz fairly, so, as Josh has gotten older, we let him assume responsibility for including Fritz in whatever we do. When we go for walks, we let Josh hold the leash; when I give Josh a cookie, I let him give Fritz a dog biscuit. However, something is not working right. Josh treats Fritz terribly. He hits him, bites him, and pulls his tail. Fortunately, Fritz is a very gentle dog, but I know it is not fair to let Josh mistreat him. The harder I try to make Josh feel important, the worse it gets. Any suggestions?*

A. This sounds like the classic case of sibling rivalry. Josh is probably very jealous of Fritz and at times would like to get rid of him.

My suggestion is that you *not* try to include Fritz in all your plans. Let Josh know that at times he will get your undivided attention. Leave Fritz at home when you go for walks. Give Josh a cookie when Fritz is not around. Put Fritz in another part of the house when you read to Josh. At times you might try letting Josh decide whether or not Fritz is included, goes along, comes into the kitchen, or gets a cookie. This will probably make him feel a little more in control and more special—which is the feeling he needs to help him overcome his jealousy.

Q. *How does a parent teach a child that more privileges also means more responsibilities? This seems especially difficult when the oldest, who has more privileges, claims to be overworked and the younger ones cry about never being allowed to "do anything."*

A. This question points up the importance of *not* trying to treat each child equally. Some parents wear themselves out trying to split everything into equal parts, spend the same amount of money on each child, buy shoes for all children whenever one needs them.

This kind of treatment promotes sibling competition and parent fatigue. I feel that it is very important for parents to treat their children as separate individuals. If possible, help each to find reasons why his position is special and unique.

Help the older child to see that, because of his position, he has certain privileges as well as certain responsibilities. Help the younger children to realize that there are some advantages as well as disadvantages to their positions.

In other words, we want our children to grow up realizing that there are certain things that they have no control over (their place in the family), and it is useless to waste energy wishing things were different. Instead, we need to teach them to devote their energies to worthwhile endeavors that will bring them satisfaction, self-esteem, pride, and happiness.

Q. *We have two children and they are as different as night and day. One is responsible, cheerful, thoughtful, and neat, while the other is the opposite. Are we doomed to accept these differences, or is there something we can do to help the second become more like the first?*

A. Most children work hard to obtain a distinctive role in the family. If one child is already adept at being "good," the other must become good at being "bad."

We can help a great deal by not comparing the two, not encouraging them to compete (in anything).

We have to be careful not to give attention to a child when he is being difficult. In other words, catch him doing something good, and heap the praise. Look for successes and help him to build on them. Find ways in which he can excel.

Q. *My six-and-a-half-year-old daughter is reluctant to try new things. She doesn't know how to ride a two-wheeler, although her friends have been riding for over a year. I have been trying to help her every day, and she always ends up in tears. This summer I made her taking swimming lessons and she got upset every day. My question is how much should I push her? She takes very little initiative and seems to drag her feet on every new task.*

A. This is always a hard decision for parents. Some children seem reluctant to try new things for fear of not being able to succeed. Maybe we need to make sure that we are not pressuring them to "be the best" or to be better than someone else. Our children pick up our attitudes early. If we are overanxious that they excel, they may be afraid of disappointing us and may give up without ever trying. Therefore, we need to take a good look at our own motives and convince them that their level of success is unimportant.

Some children do seem to need extra pushes. Maybe it would help to give her some added incentives for trying new tasks. "For every 15 minutes that you are willing to practice riding your bike, I will give you a point. When you have accumulated 10 points, I will buy you those new shorts you have been wanting."

One of our goals for children is that they learn the satisfaction that comes from investing their time and energy in constructive ways—developing new skills that will help them become more productive and competent human beings.

Q. *My two girls bicker about everything—even who gets the biggest cookie or the best-cooked bacon. I am so sick of listening to their squabbles, I could die. Is this normal?*

A. This is normal, but not necessary. There are steps that parents can take to cut down on sibling squabbling. Some suggestions are:

- Turn a deaf ear to their fights. Leave the room, if necessary, or separate the children. But do not take sides or become involved in any way.

- Reward cooperative behavior. Let them know that if they can settle their differences quietly and get along for a half hour, you will read a story or play a game with them.

- Spend time alone with each child. It is ideal if parents can take turns doing special things with their children "one on one."

If these methods don't help, as a last resort I suggest that you separate them for awhile. Do not allow them to eat breakfast, use the bathroom, or watch TV together. Most often this results in their begging to be together again. When this happens, let them begin with short amounts of time which can quickly be brought to an end if war breaks out.

Suggestions for the Week

*Try **not** to:*

1. Encourage the children to compete against each other—for anything. ("Who can drink their milk the fastest? Who can get ready for bed the quickest? Who can make the best grades?")

2. Punish both or all children for the misdeeds of one. One child gloats and the other becomes vindictive.

3. Tell one child that she should be a good example for her brother.

4. Make one child apologize to another. You are teaching him to lie. Most likely he is only sorry he got caught.

5. Put older child "in charge" of younger children. This tends to build resentment and to make the younger ones more irresponsible. If it is absolutely

necessary, it should be done rarely and only if the older child is respected by the younger ones, and if he will not flaunt his power. It is still better to put each child in charge of himself, or to have an outsider in charge of all of them.

6. Tell the older child that you expect more of him because he is older.

7. Compare the children: "Why can't you do as well as your sister? When Sara was your age, she..."

8. Expect them to be alike. "Why did you get mad at that? If I had said the same thing to your brother, he would have understood what I meant."

9. Take love for granted. Love has to be carefully taught and nurtured. It is not automatic.

10. Treat them all alike by making sure that each child gets the same number of cookies, the same size piece of cake, new shoes, or a sweater. This is not only impossible, but unrealistic.

11. Settle their arguments.

12. Get in verbal battles with them—shout, plead, scold, call names, or nag. We are teaching them to do the same.

13. In any way insinuate or imply that the way you divide your love between them will be based on who "earns" the most love.

Try to make a conscious effort to:

1. Expect your children to be different. Remember that they try not to be alike. Enjoy and accentuate their positive differences. "Lynn loves to read. Sarah loves to listen to music." Then they will not need to differ in every way. Some children deliberately lose interest in school because their brother or sister is a smashing success.

2. Treat them separately according to their differing needs. "When Janie needs new shoes, we will buy them for her. When Sally needs some, she will get them." Don't feel guilty and buy Sally something to compensate.

3. Encourage your children to excel in different areas. If one is good at piano, see if you can find another instrument for the other.

4. Ask children to make lists of things they like about their sister/ brother. Hang lists on the refrigerator door and add to them.

5. Allow and encourage children to talk about the difficulties they have with their siblings—what they do that makes them mad. Let them feel hateful. Don't shame them for their feelings. Being allowed to "talk it out" will diminish the need to "act it out."

6. Encourage dialogue between all family members. Develop the "Let's talk about it—let's make a deal" attitude. Talk over problems. Allow them to work out their own negotiations. (If your children appear to be arch-enemies, it might be wise to separate them as much as possible. Don't allow them to eat breakfast together, watch TV together. Let them earn the privilege. "One half hour of 'no fussing' time today will bring one half hour of time together in the den tomorrow.")

7. Let young children make their own "fun book" with pictures of things they like to do. Write the number of points needed to earn each privilege, and let children earn a point for each 15 minutes of cooperative behavior.

8. Praise the child's appropriate behavior. Resist the temptation to mention the opposite. Search for improvement and when you find it, praise it.

9. Reward cooperative behavior. "If you both agree at supper that the other has not been unkind to you all afternoon, we will take a ride for an ice cream cone after supper." Nobody goes if there has been a disagreement.

10. Spend qualitative time alone with each child every day. In your private talks, mention ways in which he is important to his brother or sister. Children love to take turns going out alone with a parent for special time together.

11. Reinforce thoughtful, generous, and kind behavior between your children. If it is nonexistent, try making a chart on which each child receives a point for every considerate remark and deed. Ten points earns the right to choose her favorite dinner menu.

Chapter Eight

Feelings Are Important

As we discussed in Chapter One, it is important to realize that children are people like us, with similar feelings, the same need to be recognized as important and worthwhile, and the same fear of embarrassment, humiliation, and rejection. We need to look at these feelings and learn how to handle them.

The eighth principle, then, is to recognize that feelings are important and need attention. They cannot be ignored in the hope that they will go away.

From the time a baby comes into the world, she lets us know that she has feelings and needs. At first the only way she has of telling us is by crying. The baby whose cries are not attended to either becomes more demanding and fretful, or she gives up, becomes apathetic, and withdraws into a shell.

The same is true of all of us as we get older. Our feelings don't go away but we choose different ways of handling them. Some of us become crabby, difficult, complaining, critical, or hard-to-live with. Others turn our feelings inward—

Sensitive
Parenting

171

displaying a pleasant, considerate, thoughtful, and obliging outward appearance while having a difficult time even liking ourselves. By keeping our feelings inside we can and often do become emotionally and/or physically ill.

Help Children Express Their Feelings

Mother gave six-month-old Ann a bath, then fed and changed her. Mother had housework to do, so she put Ann in her crib. After about an hour, the baby started fretting, then crying. Mother felt that her daughter was testing her and decided to ignore her, since she had a lot of work to do.

The crying persisted—and grew louder. Mother couldn't take it any longer. She went into the baby's room and slapped her child across the face. "Now shut up! Stop that crying!" Ann's cry turned into a frightened shriek.

Mother immediately felt guilty and picked the baby up. She changed her diapers and rocked her until she fell asleep.

I know there are many parents who can identify with this new mother. Babies cry for many reasons: hunger, thirst, loneliness, being soiled or wet, being gassy or overtired. Different cries are used to express different needs and these are the baby's first efforts at communication. There are times when you may not be able to recognize the signals and cannot understand why your baby is crying. At times babies are just irritable and unhappy and there doesn't seem to be a reason.

A baby's crying is never for the purpose of frustrating the parents, so we should be careful not to read intention into it. A parent should not feel guilty because a baby cries. Crying is normal.

Some babies have a difficult time falling asleep and experience a period of fussiness. It is best to put them into the crib before they are asleep, so they will become accustomed to falling asleep there. Many parents make the mistake of always rocking their first babies until they're asleep before putting them down. As these children get older they are not content to go to bed without being rocked.

Many of us also make the mistake (especially with our first babies), of entertaining them whenever they are awake. If this persists, they will come to expect attention during all their waking moments. At some period of the day it is good to withdraw—while providing toys and a stimulating environment—so that they can learn to amuse themselves and enjoy being alone.

Since crying is the only way babies have to communicate, their cries need to be responded to. They need us to spend time with them—expressing delight and pleasure in their existence. They need us to communicate with them—by touching, singing, talking, smiling—with gentle, caring, and loving messages. The more the baby is touched and held, the more secure and able to trust her environment she will become. The baby will come to see herself as she is seen in the eyes, tone of voice, manner, and attitudes of those who care for her.

Research tells us that the more consistently a baby's needs are met during the first three months, the less demanding she becomes six months later.

> Susan had been on the phone for an hour and a half, and Mother was getting more and more irritated. Finally she couldn't stand it any longer, so she went in the kitchen and yelled at Susan, "Hang up the phone this minute and come help me with dinner! Tell Jessica you have to go!"

Furious, Susan hung up and stormed to her bedroom. Mother followed, fussing at her for staying on the phone so long. Susan yelled back at her mother that she had embarrassed her in front of Jessica, her best friend. Mother told Susan that she was being silly and to come help her with dinner, but she refused and stayed in her room. When she was called to eat, Susan said that she wasn't hungry.

Mother negated Susan's feelings by telling her that she was being silly. Instead of allowing her daughter to express herself, she ignored the problem and moved on to "more important" things.

Unless we try to understand the world of the teenager, living with her can be pretty shaky and hard on parents and other family members. Many adolescents appear to be grumpy, apathetic, and indifferent. I think if we try to understand the reasons for these attitudes our lives with them will be easier.

Teenagers are busy with their own problems—and their preoccupation can immobilize them and make them insensitive to those around them. Because so much of their energy is being used up in other ways, there is very little left to exert in those areas that parents think are important.

It is very frightening for many children to give up childhood—to realize that dolls and toys are a thing of the past. Entering junior high school is another big jolt for young teens. They are often thrown in with many other children unlike themselves, who have different values, and have to decide whose values they will choose to adopt. In some junior high schools, children are tracked according to academic achievement. This may work positively for the upper third, but can be disastrous, in terms of future motivation, for the bottom two-thirds of the class.

The emerging adult-like body brings new problems to young teenagers: trying to learn the rules for heterosexual relationships and trying to decide what to do with their own sexuality. The availability of drugs and alcohol is another new option about which the adolescent must make a decision.

Somehow teenagers must resolve these conflicts. They do not need more people telling them what to do and what to believe. This is a job they must do themselves. It's no wonder that at times they're so preoccupied with the war raging inside them that they are unaware of the outside world.

The adolescent needs his friends and family. When he spends time with his friends, he is busy weighing his beliefs and values against theirs. When he is with his family, he needs support. We can help him most by "being there," listening, encouraging him to talk, and allowing for mistakes and imperfections while providing tenderness, appreciation, confidence, and love.

> Mom and Dad had gone camping overnight. Before they left, they had talked to their two sons about their plans. Mother wanted to be sure that Michael, seventeen, would be home with Stephen, thirteen. Mother asked Michael what time he would get off work. He said he would be home by midnight.
>
> When the parents returned from their trip, Stephen told them that Michael had stayed out all night.
>
> The parents were furious. They waited up for Michael, and when he came home, Dad let him have it.
>
> "What's wrong with you? Can't you ever be depended on? Where were you? Or do you know? Probably too drunk to come home. You'll never amount to anything—I give up on you! We're not good enough for you anymore, are we? Why don't you just move out! See how well you can do on your own."
>
> Michael stormed out of the house. He never had a chance to explain. His parents did not learn where he had been or why he had not come home. With the lecture his dad gave him, the chances are slim that he would feel like telling them.

Although our children disappoint us at times and fail to honor our wishes, when we deny them the chance to explain themselves, berate them, or make them feel small, we deprive them of the incentive to do better and become more responsible.

We need to separate the child from his deeds. Although we can be disappointed in his decisions and actions, we cannot afford to convey the message that we give up on him, for then he may give up on himself, turning our words of doom into a self-fulfilling prophecy.

> Susan, fifteen, and Doug, seventeen, were talking at the table when their father asked, "Doug, did you get the car inspected today?"
>
> Doug looked up, but did not answer. He continued his conversation with Susan.

"Doug, your father asked you a question," said Mother, who was serving dinner.

"Well, I was talking to Susan, Mom. Dad interrupted our conversation."

"Did you, or did you not get the car inspected, son?"

"I did not," Doug said.

"You didn't? Why not? I thought I told you to get it inspected," Father said. "Don't you ever listen to me anymore? I hope you weren't planning to use the car tonight, because you're not going anywhere. If you can't do as you're told, you can just consider yourself grounded."

"Hey, wait a minute," Doug said. "That's not fair. I have a date and need the car. I couldn't help it that I ran out of time today. That's what I hate. You just issue orders without knowing the facts."

"Jerry, I don't think you're being fair to Doug," Mother said. "He has a date with Phyllis, and she can't help it if he didn't get the car inspected. I'm sure he'll do it tomorrow. Won't you Doug?"

"Yeah, sure, Mom, but Dad's already said I can't have the car. He never listens." Doug threw his fork down and left the table.

"Doug, come back here and finish your dinner," Dad ordered.

"You were too hard on him, Jerry. I'm sure he'll get the car inspected tomorrow."

"You always stick up for him. I don't know why I bother with these kids," Father said. "You never back me up. That's why they won't ever listen to me!"

Susan finished her meal quickly and left the table, while her parents ate in silence.

When Doug was ready to go out, he borrowed his mother's keys, saying nothing to his father.

"What time are you coming in, son?" his father asked. Doug answered by slamming the door.

Mother and Dad said little to each other all evening.

Communication skills in this family are sadly lacking. There was no open dialogue between Doug and his father. The boy was not given the chance to explain why he had not gotten the car inspected. His father issued an ultimatum before he knew the facts.

Then Mother stepped in and defended Doug by telling her husband he was being unfair. Doug must have known her word was final. He was allowed to disobey his father and take the car.

It is important for parents to present a united front. If they disagree, they should discuss it in private and reach a mutual agreement.

When children can pit their parents against each other, no one wins. Friction between the adults mounts and the child loses respect for both. He develops the attitude that he can override authority, and this often results in rebellion, carelessness, insensitivity, and irresponsibility.

Children Need Help with Their Fears

Gail, two, had fallen on a toy while running down the hall at home, and her mouth had bled profusely. Mother discovered that her daughter's upper front tooth was missing. She phoned her husband to come home and help, knowing that the tooth could be reimplanted if they found it and got her to the dentist in time. Finally they gave up the search and both parents took her to the dentist's office. The father had a history of fainting at the sight of blood, so he waited outside. Mother became extremely anxious. She was shaking so much that she couldn't hold the child. Gail was uncontrollably frightened, and the dentist had to use a restraining device even to see in her mouth. Finally he asked Mother to wait in the outside office.

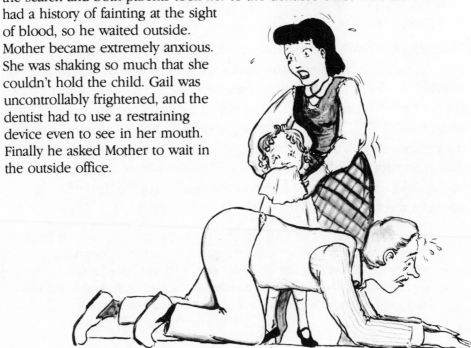

Gail picked up her parents' fear and anxiety and became hysterical. Compared to her fear, her pain was short-lived. The dentist's need to restrain Gail to look in her mouth only added to her anxiety and made her less cooperative. He finally found that her fall had pushed her tooth up into her gum. She was no longer in pain; her hysteria was from fear.

Fears are learned and children learn most of them from their parents. They are transmitted by mannerisms, over-cautiousness, and over-protection, as well as by words and actions. A certain amount of fear is necessary for survival, but an overabundance can stunt growth, interfere with learning, and make a child antisocial.

Babies begin life feeling omnipotent, but as their awareness increases, they begin to realize they are not actually in control of everything, and start to become fearful. By the time a child is seven or eight months old, it is not uncommon for her to begin to be wary of unfamiliar objects and people. As she develops, the content of her fears changes. When she is about two, she may become fearful of vacuum cleaners, hair dryers, and toilets, and suspicious of what they might do to her. (Since she is becoming aware of her own angry feelings, she attributes to inanimate objects the same motives that she has lurking beneath the surface.)

Because children have trouble separating reality from fantasy, preschoolers take on imaginary and symbolic fears such as ghosts, monsters, and witches. Many of these seem irrational, illogical, and absurd to the observing bystander. By the time children reach school age, their fears are more realistic: floods, tornadoes, fires, burglaries, illness, and kidnappers. Because they are still egocentric, they cannot understand probability and feel that every catastrophe they hear about will happen to them. Children's fears subside as they mature and develop, and become more competent and able to deal with the potential dangers, threats, and hazards of the outside world.

> Five-year-old Wesley and his father were walking hand-in-hand through a very crowded zoo. They saw an hysterical mother talking with a policeman, describing her daughter who had wandered away and was lost. The woman was sobbing loudly, almost uncontrollably, and was hardly able to talk. Wesley asked his father what was wrong.

Father proceeded to tell Wesley that the lady had lost her little girl because she had not held her mother's hand like she was supposed to. He dramatically explained that the missing child was alone in a strange place where many bad things could happen to her. She could be run over by a car and killed or could be pulled into a cage by a wild animal and eaten.

He then pointed out that even if these terrible things did not happen, the lost child might never find her mother and might be alone in the world forever. He concluded with a very stern and emphatic warning that the same thing could happen to Wesley if he did not obey his father.

Wesley became very apprehensive and began clinging to his father. Soon he wanted to be carried. His father refused, saying that Wesley was much too big for that type of thing. Then Wesley began crying that he wanted to go home.

After listening to his pleading and whining for more than an hour, Wesley's dad finally gave up and left the zoo, disgusted with his son and vowing that he would never bring him back to the zoo again.

Wesley's father thought that witnessing this scene would impress his son with the dangers of a strange place and the consequences of not doing what he was told. He did not realize, however, that instead of making Wesley cautious and careful, he was terrifying him, and the end result was scaring the child into believing the same thing would happen to him. He became so obsessed with the fear of getting lost that he was no longer able to enjoy the zoo's attractions.

The father could have explained that the woman's child was lost, assured his son that the policeman would help her find the little girl, and reminded him that because of the large crowd and unfamiliar surroundings, it was important for them to stay together.

This could have been an excellent opportunity to talk with his son, asking him where he thought the child might have gone, how he thought the child would feel, and how the mother was going to feel when she found the child. It would also have been a good time to discuss how kind policemen are and all the ways in which they are able to help lost children.

Well-meaning adults can unintentionally instill unwarranted fears in children by exaggerating facts to make a point. Children have such imaginations that they can quickly build a tiny fear into a grand-sized phobia that can cause problems for years to come.

Fear is an easy motivator or deterrent for little children (Wesley's father had no trouble convincing his son to hold his hand), but can also petrify and paralyze a child until he is no longer free to enjoy the simple pleasures of life that most of us take for granted.

> Chris, four, eagerly raced ahead of his father on his way to a very tall slide. When he got up close, he hesitated. "Go on," called his dad. "I'm watching." The child turned toward his father and shook his head "no."
>
> "Go on," said his father as he too approached the slide. "Don't be a sissy. You're a big boy now." Chris continued to resist, and his father tried to encourage him with such statements as: "Look at the other children. They're not afraid. See how much fun they're having? You'll like it. Go on. Just try it! We came here for you to have fun, now go on!"

When Chris began to cry, his father called him a sissy, yanked him by the arm, and took him out of the park as if he, the father, had lost face.

What might have been an enjoyable time together turned into a disaster, and the relationship between father and son suffered a major breakdown. Father humiliated his child and tried to make him feel guilty about not living up to his expectations.

Instead of judging the child's character and personality, or trying to change his mind, the father needed to address himself to the child's situation. The negative shake of the child's head was a call for help. The father needed to understand his son's message and accept his feelings. "You don't want to go on the slide now? Is it too high? It seems higher up close than it did from a distance, doesn't it?"

This way the child feels accepted and respected. He is taken seriously and not blamed and ridiculed. When a parent is accepting of a child's feelings, the child often gathers strength to cope.

The father might have tried to reduce the child's fear by gradually increasing his exposure to the situation while the child was comfortable, relaxed, and secure. He could have held his son in his lap and silently watched the other children. They could have played in the sandbox or enjoyed some other activity.

On another day, the father might suggest holding the boy on the bottom on the slide to let him feel what the tail end of the ride would be like—or climb with him part way up the ladder just for the view.

Later the father might suggest sliding down with his son in his lap (being careful to back off if his son declined). Approached in this way, the child may eventually take the initiative to slide down by himself.

We often have the mistaken notion that we should or must talk our children out of their fears. We fail to recognize that the best way to help is by providing them with an atmosphere where they are free to master new obstacles when they feel like it and where they will not suffer shame when they lack the courage to do so.

Nine-year-old twins Dean and David were looking around in the shopping center with five-year-old brother Marc while Mother was shopping. They had to use the bathroom, and found one in a drug store. The older boys decided to play a trick on Marc. When they went out, they locked the bathroom door from the outside so he couldn't get out. They stayed nearby and heard him scream for them to come open the door. They finally opened it, but not before he was terrified and embarrassed.

The outcome of this incident was that Marc developed an intense fear of public bathrooms. For several years he would avoid using one if at all possible. If he did have to use one, he would insist that his mother hold her foot in the door so that it could not close.

Many children have a fear of public bathrooms. Sometimes it is because they have had a bad experience. Perhaps, like Marc, they have been locked in by mistake or by a prankster. Maybe the door jammed or stuck and they were afraid they couldn't get out, or someone jumped out at them and scared them, or turned off the lights and left them in the dark. Many times we never know what caused the fright. Sometimes the child himself may not even remember, or may not be able to talk about it.

Children learn many of their fears through upsetting and frightening experiences. Adults who have abnormal fears of animals, heights, closed-in places, or water are often able to trace their fears back to childhood experiences.

It is helpful if we can recognize fear in children, so that we can help them overcome it, if possible, or at least cope with it in a constructive way.

There are four basic ways in which people show fear:

1. visibly, by crying, screaming, shaking, or running away;

2. freezing in panic;

3. exaggerated fascination, unending questions, and insatiable desire to repeat experiences; and

4. apparent disinterest—unconcerned exterior, complete lack of emotion.

Obviously some of these ways make it easy for us to detect fear, but others are deceiving. It is important to be aware of the many ways fear can be manifested.

Most fears will go away in time, as the child becomes more able to comprehend reality and exercise control over his environment. There are steps we can take, however, to help the process along. First of all, we should be careful *not* to make fun of or shame the child. We should not become impatient or force him to face the things he fears. We should:

1. Encourage the child to talk freely about his fear.

2. Provide opportunities for dramatic play, or drawing and painting, to help him re-create his scary feelings and experiences, so that he will be able to identify and master them.

3. Try to determine the origin of the fear, so that, if possible, it can be removed or at least dealt with.

4. Strengthen the child's coping strategies. Give him as much information as possible, so that he can deal with it ahead of time. (Explain what is going to take place—don't spring surprises.) Give the child opportunities to practice solving problems and using alternative behaviors. ("What would you do if you were lost... if you got hurt... if you had to get a shot? What else could you do?")

5. Give him opportunities to become accustomed to potentially frightening situations a little at a time, in smaller, less threatening forms (pictures of dogs, small backyard pools, doctor's kits).

6. Make sure that the child's expressions of fear are not being reinforced. Provide the warmth and comfort he needs at other times, so that he does not have to express a fear to receive attention.

If these methods do not help and if the child's fear persists to the extent that he is incapacitated by it, it would be wise to seek professional help (such as that found in child guidance or mental health clinics). When the cause of the anxiety is uncovered, the child will then be free to turn his newly released energy into more useful channels.

Unexpressed Anger Can Cripple

Three-year-old Randy was throwing toys all over the yard while his father was trying to mow the lawn. His dad yelled at him to stop throwing the toys and start picking them up. Randy looked at his father and said, "no."

Father stopped his mowing and said, "Don't you say 'no' to me." Then he sat Randy down on top of the picnic table. "You stay right there." As he walked away, Randy called after him, "You're mean!"

His dad walked back to the picnic table and said, "What did you say? What did you call me?"

Randy mumbled, "Nothing."

"Yes, you did!" shouted his dad and slapped Randy on the face. "Now, what did you say?" Instead of answering, Randy started crying.

"I said, what did you say?" repeated his father, as he slapped Randy on the other side of his face. Then he pointed his finger at Randy and said, "I don't care if you don't like me. You're going to straighten up."

He turned his back and started to walk away. Before he got very far, he turned back around and shouted, "I'd better not hear another peep out of you! You'd better straighten up and stop that crying. What are you, a sissy? I'll deal with you later."

This is a good example of the mishandling of anger. Randy's father quickly forgot the business at hand (picking up the toys) and spent his energies trying to punish his son for being angry.

Randy's dad could have helped Randy a great deal if he could have expressed his real feelings to him. "I need you to pick up your toys. When you throw your toys around the yard, they get lost and broken. I can't cut the grass when they're in the way, and that makes me angry. When I ask you to help and you say 'no' it makes me mad. It would help me if you would pick the toys up and put them by the back door. Come on, I'll help you."

He could also accept Randy's feelings by saying, "I can understand that it is more fun to throw toys than to pick them up, and I can also understand that it makes you mad for me to ask you to help. I'm sorry, but I need your help."

Neither slapping his son nor making him sit on the table got the toys picked up or taught Randy a lesson in responsibility. Instead, father and son became engaged in a power struggle, which neither of them won.

Anger is an emotion that most of us find difficult to handle. In fact, many of us try to deny its existence. But anger is here to stay. Anger is a part of life.

Anger can be an energizer—a motivating force that moves us to make changes and take action, but it can also cripple, maim, and drain us of enthusiasm and zest for life. What we *do* with anger is the important issue.

I believe there are five ways to handle anger—from the most immature and unhealthy to the most healthy. The first is turning it inward. This is the child who doesn't respond at all. He dislikes himself, maybe bites himself, or pulls his hair, or maybe he can't think of anything good about himself. He turns it inward. This can become illness: asthma, stomach problems, cancer. Of course the extreme form of this self-hate is suicide. We certainly don't want our children to hate themselves, but if we tell them to deny their anger, sometimes that's the only recourse they have. Turning it inward is the worst choice they can make.

The second way to handle anger is to turn it outward. Aim it toward someone else—hit back, lash out. We can lash out physically, psychologically, and emotionally. You hit me, I'm going to hit you. A lot of spanking and hurting of children is retaliation. And the reason children lash out is because they've been hurt. We hit them, they hit somebody else. So lashing out at somebody else is also not the best outlet. It is an unhealthy and counterproductive way to deal with anger.

A third way to express anger is to choose a non-productive outlet: kick a box, hit a punching bag, throw rocks, slam a door, break glassware, or knock over a table with all the dishes on it. I had a student who went into her husband's closet when she was mad at him and threw all his clothes out on the floor. When that wasn't enough, she slashed his best pants. That's all rather non-productive!

The fourth choice is to find a productive outlet like jogging, baking bread, painting, cleaning house, scrubbing, playing the piano, or playing tennis. We can think of lots of these! They are all excellent outlets for anger. When you have a lot of adrenalin and energy, you can get a lot done. It's a good, healthy way to vent anger.

But the fifth—and most important—one (and the only one that really removes the anger) is *talking.* Verbalize it. This has to be done at the right time, with the right person and place. Be careful who you talk to, when you talk, and how you say it. Sometimes it's helpful to find a productive outlet first—go run around the block while you're thinking about it.

It took me two months to get up enough nerve to decide how I was going to confront my boss with something that was really getting to me and causing me to be ill. I had a lot of support and help from people who said, "Look, this is what you suggest for others—you've got to do it." So I chose the place—a restaurant—where he couldn't yell at me. I invited him to lunch. I planned it all: the right time, the right place, the right person. I wrote my speech and memorized it and I asked him to meet me there. (Of course he didn't show up on time, and I felt sure he wasn't coming.) When he finally arrived, I just blurted it out. He looked at me—stunned—and said, "You should have told me months ago." He was sincere. I was thrown off guard—I was expecting him to blow up, to get mad, to threaten my job, but it all turned out beautifully.

It is important that we teach our children to express their anger in healthy ways so that it will not remain inside them to become a destructive force in their lives.

> It was Sunday morning and Mother was late getting breakfast because five-year-old Tommy's brother and sister were both sick and required her attention. Tommy went into the kitchen and found a bag of brownies, which he carried into the bedroom and announced he was going to eat. Mother explained that the brownies were for dessert after lunch and suggested that Tommy either get himself a bowl of cereal or wait a few minutes until she could fix him an egg. Tommy insisted on brownies.

> Mother grabbed the brownies out of Tommy's hand, took them into the kitchen and hid them on a top shelf. She returned to the bedroom to find Tommy threatening his little sister, Carole, with a large toy in his hand. He yelled to Mother that he was going to throw it unless she let him have a brownie.

> Frightened, Mother started after Tommy and chased him through the den, into the kitchen, and back to the bedroom. Just as she was about to reach him, he pitched the toy through the air and it hit the wall, making a dent and knocking a picture to the floor.

> Mother was very angry. She grabbed Tommy and spanked him hard, telling him how bad he was and how much trouble he had caused

her—especially when the other two children were sick. After the spanking, she made him go to his room and told him that he could just forget about breakfast—and brownies too—for that matter.

It is not uncommon for a healthy child to feel left out when the others have been sick. Many times that child will look for ways to demand extra attention. Tommy seized an opportunity to defy Mother by threatening to eat the brownies, and then, when he was stopped, to hurt his sister.

The ending of this story could have been quite different if Mother had reacted in another manner. She might have calmly tried to figure out what the real problem was and acknowledged Tommy's feelings ("I understand that you are very angry. So angry, in fact, that you would like to throw that toy at Carole. I would like to talk with you about it as soon as you are ready.")

When a child's anger escalates to violence, it is helpful if the parent will recognize the emotion behind the act and verbalize that recognition. ("I'm sure that you would like to hurt your sister and maybe hurt me too. It must have been tough these last several days when your brother and sister were sick and I had to spend so much time with them. I missed spending time with you.") Just helping a child accept his negative feelings and letting him know that you understand is often a remedy in itself, and makes any further action unnecessary.

The brownies were not the issue. The real issue was a test on Tommy's part to check out his importance and to demand equal time from Mother. He baited her and she fell for it.

We should avoid confrontations with our children at all costs, because someone has to back down. Whoever it is will most likely retreat and regroup until he can find another way to aggravate, exasperate, or retaliate. Children need mature parents who demonstrate composure and compassion, and who help them save face and recover when they have lost control.

Parents Need To Tell It Like It Is

The family had made plans to go to the movies together. After dinner, father and the two teenage children went in the den and turned on the TV. Mother, resentful that no one offered to help with the dishes, hurried around in the kitchen, banging dishes and slamming cabinet doors. The children heard her and started giggling. She stormed into the den and asked, "What's so funny?" They got quiet and didn't answer. Father said, "When will you be ready? I wish you'd hurry. The movie starts in twenty minutes." Mother replied sharply, "I'm doing the best I can." The next thing her husband heard was the back door slamming, and he realized that she had gone to feed the dogs. To the children he muttered, "We may as well forget the movie. We've already missed the first show."

By the time Mother was finally ready, Father and both children were in bad moods. Mother felt angry, hurt, and resentful. No one had offered to help her and she had done all the work herself. She thought it served them right to be late for the show.

Mother would be happier if she could learn to express her needs. "I need some help in the kitchen. If you will pitch in, we can get to the movie sooner. The dishes need to be washed, the kitchen swept, and the dogs fed." So often we expect our families to know what we want and then assume that they are being thoughtless, lazy, or selfish. We will find that when we talk honestly with them about our needs, they will be much more willing to help.

Parenting is a never-ending, difficult, time-consuming task, which takes a great deal of energy and often produces heartaches and gray hairs. Many women were taught that being feminine meant being modest, compliant, self-effacing, supportive, sensitive, and intuitive. We learned these traits early in life, and indeed they come in handy when we need to offer nurturance and warmth to our children.

However, there is a danger that if we always look out for the needs of others, we will become frustrated, isolated, and depleted. Worse yet, we may even lose touch with our own identity and needs. Since we think that it is not our right to speak up for ourselves, we often resort to subversive tactics to get our way. We learn early to become silent, moody, mysterious, tearful, or manipulative when we are unhappy. We resort to scolding, threatening, yelling, arguing, nagging, lecturing, accusing, blaming, or begging. We become our children's servants. We fuss and complain, and in turn they "tune us out" and become disrespectful. In order to gain the respect of our children, we would do well to learn to express our feelings, to take responsibility for letting them know how we feel and what we expect. In short, we need to learn to say:

> I **need** (some help with the dishes)
> I **want** (you to call me if you are going to be late)
> I **feel** (embarrassed when you and your sister pick at each other in public)
> I **like** (it when you get up when you're called)
> I **don't want** (to pick up your dirty clothes)
> I **don't like** (it when you talk ugly to me)
> I **don't feel** (it's fair for you to leave dirty dishes in the den)

We should remember that the people in our families aren't mind-readers. When we are honest and open about our needs, wants, likes, and feelings, and when we make our expectations clear, we find that the reward is increasing love, concern, and cooperation.

> Father had come home from a frustrating day at work. Things had not gone well at the office, his secretary was out sick, and traffic was terrible. When he got home, he was tired and sat down with a drink to read the newspaper. Chip, three, who was excited to see his daddy, came into the den with a book. He sidled up to Daddy's chair and said,

"Here, Daddy, read to me." His father didn't pay any attention. Chip pushed gently on the newspaper, repeating his request. His father still didn't listen to him. Chip pushed hard on the newspaper and yelled, "Here, Daddy, read to me!" Without realizing it, he pushed Daddy's drink out of his hand, causing it to spill on the floor.

Daddy was angry. "Can't you leave me alone? Don't you see that I'm reading the paper? See what you made me do?'"

Chip felt terrible. He left the room crying.

Daddy had a right to his tired and frustrated feelings. If he had taken the time to tell Chip that he needed a few minutes to himself because he had had a hard day, Chip could have known that he was not to blame. As it was, Chip left feeling that he had caused trouble for his father. Parents should realize that they have a right to their feelings and also that children are entitled to know what those feelings are. This makes for a safer climate and a more relaxed home environment.

Elizabeth, nineteen, was lying in the back yard in the sun. She had been there about half an hour, when Mother came outside.

"Elizabeth, would you like to go with me to the grocery store? I need some things for dinner."

"No, Mom. I want to get some sun and this is the only hot day we've had this week."

Mother went back in the house slamming the door behind her. In a few minutes, Elizabeth heard Mother leave in the car.

Later, when Elizabeth offered to help set the table, Mother snapped, "No thanks. I'll do it myself." Dinner was eaten in silence. When Elizabeth left to go out, she thanked Mother for the dinner. Mother said nothing.

Obviously Mother wanted Elizabeth to go with her to the grocery store and was disappointed when she chose to stay home. However, she phrased the question in such a way that Elizabeth thought she was free to make a choice.

Mother would have been more honest if she had said, "I would like to have a chance to be with you this afternoon. I need some groceries. Would you ride with me to the store?"

Elizabeth might have been willing to sacrifice her own needs (to lie in the sun) for those of her mother, or, if not, at least she could have dealt with the real issue, and perhaps compromised. "I'd really like to get some sun. Could we go a little later?"

When we ask someone if she "wants" to do something, we are implying that she is free to say "no." However, if we have a stake in the outcome, if we are hoping she will say "yes," we are setting ourselves up for disappointment by giving her an option. It is not fair to punish her if her choice is not what we would like.

We should not expect our children to always know what we want. If we don't teach them by example to express their needs, they will likewise have difficulty speaking up for themselves.

It takes determination and practice to develop the skills of open communication. The rewards are well worth the effort, however, for we are spared the pain of unnecessary guessing games, guilt trips, moods, and disappointments.

Relationships bloom and flourish in an atmosphere where people are able and free to express their wants and needs in ways that are clear and honest. When others are not expected to guess the "hidden message" they are more willing to sacrifice their own desires on behalf of those they love.

Thomas Gordon in his "Effectiveness Training" teaches the useful tool of "I-Messages." He suggests that the first step in problem-solving is to decide "who owns the problem?" This is easily determined by asking, "Who is it bugging?" If it is bugging you, you own the problem, and if you own it, then it is up to you to do something about it. If you decide that it is not your problem, then you can ignore it. For example, if your child's messy room bothers you, you have a choice: either decide not to let it bother you or take the initiative to find a solution.

If you decide to make it your problem, then Gordon suggests that you use an "I-Message" to state your case. He explains that an "I-Message" contains three parts: 1) the behavior or what's happening, 2) the effect it has on you, and 3) how you feel about it. For example, "When you don't clean up your room (behavior), we have to look at the mess (effect), and I feel resentful (feeling)."

Most of us hope that other people will solve our problems for us. We huff around, or we get in moods, or sulk, hoping that someone else will notice and take action. This rarely works, first because other people have their own problems to solve, and second, because they become resentful when they feel that someone is trying to manipulate them.

An "I-Message" is an honest, up-front way of handling the situation. It is amazing how effective it can be. At first the other person is usually stunned—he is not accustomed to having people talk to him like this, and it takes awhile for it to sink in. After the initial shock, however, *if the relationship is good,* there is usually a change in the other person's behavior. It might not be right away. Frequently, the other person says nothing, but if you wait, you will probably see him take some steps to change his behavior. Of course, the change may only be temporary, but at least there is a change, and you can work from there. You have opened up honest dialogue which is healthy and useful, and can be a stepping stone to a permanent solution.

One of my graduate students went home from class and delivered an "I-Message" to her two daughters—ages sixteen and nine. "I have a problem when I come home from class and the kitchen is a mess. I have to use my time to clean up instead of being able to spend time with you. I feel angry having to give up this time which is really important to me." The girls said nothing in response, but the next night when she arrived home, the dishes were in the dishwasher and the food was put away.

An "I-Message" often has that kind of effect on people. Their initial response is silence or surprise, but after they have had time to think about it, they decide to change their behavior.

Another mother was helping her daughter with homework while working at the kitchen table. The child was twisting the toe of her sock while she was listening. "Katie, I am having a problem. When I am helping you with your addition and you twist the toe of your sock, it distracts me so I can't think about the math, and I feel frustrated." Her daughter stared at her mother in silence and stopped twisting her sock.

"When you ride your bike without telling me, I don't know where you are, and I'm afraid something might happen to you," another mother told her nine-year-old son late one afternoon. "Gee, Mom," he replied, after an initial silence, "I forgot to let you know where I was going. I'm sorry."

A mother of a four-year-old decided to try an "I-Message" on her little boy when she was distracted by his behavior at dinner. "Matthew, I have a problem. When you lie across your chair while you're eating your dinner, I'm afraid that you will choke on your food, and that makes me upset." Matthew sat up and finished his dinner. He never said a word.

When we bottle up our feelings and can't speak up for ourselves, or when we let other people take advantage of us, we become resentful, hostile, or even physically sick. If we can get it out—talk about it, own up to our feelings—then we're free. We have more energy, more enthusiasm. We don't have a need to prove ourselves. We can affirm those we love!

Questions and Answers

Q. *My four-year-old has suddenly begun to fear the dark. She will not go upstairs alone and begs to keep her light on at night. Her father thinks this is ridiculous and says we should not give in to her. I feel caught in the middle. What do you think?*

A. It's natural for children this age to suddenly be afraid of things. We should help them through this difficult period. Some suggestions are:

1. Allow her to keep a night light on as long as she asks for it.

2. Let her keep a flashlight near the bed.

3. Invite a friend over to spend the night—one who is not afraid of the dark.

4. Sit on her bed with the lights out and talk, sing, tell pleasant stories, or rub her back.

5. Don't be disappointed in her. Let her know the fear is common among children and that she will probably outgrow it.

Q. *My five-year-old daughter seems very insecure. All of a sudden, she does not want me out of her sight. She wants to know where I am all the time, and if I go out, she wants me to leave a telephone number where she can reach me. She calls me every half hour and if she can't reach me, she starts calling my friends. It is embarrassing, and I feel foolish that I have to obey her curfews. Should I give in to her demands, or should I just ignore her protests?*

A. Children have many fears that they may or may not be able to express. One of the most prevalent ones is that of separation from their loved ones (by death, accidents, or kidnapping). Most experts agree that these fears are very real and should not be minimized by trying to convince the child that the fears are ungrounded or silly.

Children need the right to be afraid and an atmosphere in which they can express their fears and try to deal with them. Otherwise they might be forced to submerge them, causing undue stress and anxiety. As they grow mentally and physically, and begin to master their environment, we hope they will be able to put their fears into better perspective.

I think if you will be patient and leave numbers where you can be reached for a while, she will soon outgrow this need.

Q. *I am ten-years-old and in the fifth grade. I'm tall for my age and look funny in socks. I want to wear hose, but if I say anything about it in front of my dad, he'll have a fit. All the other girls in my class wear hose with dresses. The girls at church do too. I hate having to wear socks. I look much better in hose. Can you help me?*

A. Your dad probably feels that if he allows you to wear hose, you'll grow up too fast and expect to do other things that older children are doing. It is sometimes difficult for parents to see their children doing and wanting things that were different from when they were growing up. But they should understand that just like when they were young, you want to "look right" and dress like your friends—at least enough so you don't "stick out" by being different.

How you feel about yourself is very important. I suggest that you tell your dad that you have something to discuss with him when he has time. Try to be very pleasant and respectful. You might write it out ahead of time, so you will say it exactly the way you want. Try to assure him that you want to obey him and honor his wishes, but that you don't feel very good about yourself when you look different from your friends. Offer to make a deal—"If you will let me wear stockings with dresses, I will cook you a special meal, or I will get up a half hour earlier and straighten my room, or wash the breakfast dishes before I leave for school each morning."

Most parents want to see their children become more responsible and dependable. If you can convince him that you are growing up in other ways, too, he might be willing to change his mind.

Q. *Our son (age fourteen) is very sarcastic and rude to adults. At a recent church picnic, I was embarrassed by his language and his attitude. How much of this obnoxious behavior is to be expected of a child of this age?*

A. I don't think we need to accept rude behavior from children. First we should make sure that they are not imitating *our* rude behavior (to them). Then we should talk with them about it ("I'm embarrassed when you are rude."). If this doesn't help, we might offer to make a deal. "Each day that you go without saying anything rude, I will fix you a special snack before bedtime." Children often need a little push in order to break a bad habit, and parents can facilitate the needed change by offering the necessary incentives.

Q. *What punishment is effective for a fifteen-year-old boy? I'm ready to throw in the towel. Everything I try seems to backfire. If I tell him to go to his room, he is happy to go. If I put him on restriction, it makes him sullen, angry, defiant, and impossible to live with. Besides, I would have to stay home twenty-four hours a day to enforce it.*

*He can find more excuses why he **has** to go somewhere, and I finally give up and forget the restriction. His father threatens to take the belt to him but we can both see that this only makes matters worse. We are at our wit's end.*

A. For the reasons you mentioned, and more, I feel that the best approach with teenagers is not punishment and restriction. Most children will react (or want to) in the same manner as your son—with more hostility, anger, resentment, and retaliation.

I believe that honest, open dialogue is the best answer.

"Son, I need to talk with you. I am not happy with our relationship. I am not happy with some of the things you do, and I know you do not like some of the things we do. I want us to work out some arrangements and agreements where we both will feel better."

"I don't feel that the way I have been handling things in the past has worked. It has not helped us to be closer or for you to want to obey us. I am willing to try some new approaches. How would you like it if we make some deals? You make a list of some of the things you would like for us to do for you or privileges you would like. We will see if we can work out ways for you to earn these things by doing jobs and being more accountable and responsible with your life" (being ready on time, respectful to adults, keeping your room straight—whatever).

If you have not been in the habit of talking with your son this way, it will be hard at first—for both of you. But don't give up. It gets easier. At first he may act as if he isn't listening. Don't be fooled. When he sees that you really mean it and that you are willing to get off his back (stop nagging, scolding, fussing, reminding) he will probably like the new arrangement quite well.

Children (of all ages) want better relationships with their parents—but it is up to the parents to initiate them.

Q. *I have only been married two years, but my husband's sixteen-year-old daughter has decided that she wants to live with us. I am shaky about her coming, because we have never gotten along very well. I feel that she is jealous of my intrusion in her life—maybe blames me for taking her father away from her. I know my husband wants us to get along, but I'm not sure it's possible. Should I tell him I don't think it will work, or should I try it?*

A. This is a real tough situation—one which has no easy answers. My suggestion is to level with everyone. Tell your husband exactly how you feel, and if possible, talk very openly with his daughter also. Encourage her to talk. It may be that once the air is cleared, you will be able to understand each other a little better and will not be playing guessing games about where you stand with her. It is much easier to deal with the known than it is to try to deal with the unknown.

Tell her how shaky you feel because you are not her mother and know you cannot take her mother's place. Tell her that you want to play a different role in her life—but you will have to feel your way along and need her help.

If she does move in, try to establish strong lines of honest, two-way communication from the beginning. Know that there will be bumpy roads, but try to make them stepping stones to a workable and comfortable relationship between you.

Q. *My teenage daughter never wants to go anywhere with us any more. I still want our family to do things together, but she can always think up an excuse for not going with us. It really hurts my feelings. I tell her not to go if she doesn't want to be with us, and then she chooses to stay home or go out with her friends. I would like for her to **want** to be with us. Is this too much to ask?*

A. Teenagers are preoccupied with their own wishes, problems, and concerns, and give little thought to the needs of others, especially those of their family. However, I don't think we should back down and let them do only what they want. It is our responsibility as adults to *teach* our children to be concerned and sensitive to the needs of others. I would suggest some dialogue and some bargains with your daughter. "Since it is so important to me that we do some things together as a family, I am willing to make a deal with you. If you will go (pleasantly) out to eat with us tomorrow night, you will be free to invite some of your friends over Friday night for pizza.

Give your child plenty of notice when you want her to do something special with you. Let her know exactly what you expect. I have found that when children have enough time to prepare themselves mentally for an ordeal that they may find to be unpleasant, they are much more agreeable and fun to have around. Make sure that family times are pleasant (no lectures, fights, or unending, repetitious, and boring monologues).

Q. *My twenty-year-old daughter is home for the summer. We have always gotten along well, but it seems that this summer we are arguing over everything. I can't figure out what's wrong. I feel like I can't please her. Is this normal, or do I need some counseling?*

A. It might help you to understand what she is going through: the need to separate from her family and become her own person. When children have been away at school and have become accustomed to making their own decisions, it is often difficult for them to return to the home setting and fit into the family again.

Talking it out would probably help and maybe a third party would be able to be more objective.

Suggestions for the Week

1. Engage your family in dialogue. Ask each person to tell "What I like most about my family."

2. Ask each family member to write on a piece of paper, "The things that make me the angriest about my family."

3. Ask each person to tell what he *used* to be afraid of.

4. Ask them to tell what they are afraid of now.

5. Ask each person in the family to reflect on one time he was embarrassed earlier in life. Encourage him to tell it verbatim, as accurately as he can remember it.

6. Have each family member list five things that embarrass him now or make him angry. Encourage each one to elaborate as much as possible—without negating any feelings. ("That's silly" or "You shouldn't feel that way.")

7. Ask each person to try to decide what he does when he is mad. Be honest yourself, and try to look at behavior you have used to cope with anger.

8. Try to put together an "I-Message." Include the behavior that bothers you, the effect that behavior has on you, and how you feel about it. Deliver your "I-Message" to the person you wrote it to. Watch to see if there is any change in the behavior.

9. Practice starting sentences with "I feel," "I like," "I need," "I would appreciate it if you would . . ." Encourage your family to do the same. When they express themselves to you, learn to listen with caring and concern, and try to openly acknowledge the feelings they are expressing, without becoming defensive and judgmental.

10. Plan for weekly family meetings during which each member is given a chance to discuss his concerns and problems.

Chapter Nine

Parents Are Models

In the final analysis, the strongest influence on a child is the way his parents live their own lives. Since the child is first influenced by those who care for him, they shape his life in more ways than they realize or even wish for. Even if the child later rebels and chooses to take on characteristics that are opposite to those of his parents, it is still, in fact, the parents who had the greatest influence in shaping him.

The ninth principle, then, is to be careful to exhibit the behaviors we expect our children to develop and incorporate into their own lives—to be models of what we wish them to become.

We can learn a lot about ourselves by watching our children. Very early, we see them hold their fork like we do, stand the same way, walk the same way, and use the same inflections in their voices. We would be wise to take a look at our own behaviors and work to change those we don't want our children to copy.

It is important that we be honest—both verbally and non-verbally—with our children. They can sense early on whether or not we are sincere, if we mean what we say, say what we mean, and "practice what we preach."

Children need parents who are confident and willing to back up what they say with action. Even though our children may challenge our decisions and cause us to doubt ourselves at times, they need to know that we, who are older and wiser, have their best interests at heart and will require them to respect and obey us.

Parents do not need to be perfect. In fact, children have to learn that there is uncertainty, ambivalence, and imperfection in life. What they need to learn from us is how to cope: how to solve problems, make choices, look at alternatives, and learn from mistakes. Children need parents who are conscientiously trying to get their own acts together. Then, and only then, can they grow up knowing that when disappointments and trouble come, help is available.

Children Will Imitate Their Parents

Josh, five, had gone down the street to play with a friend. He told his mother where he was going and when he would be back. When he got home, she was not there. There was no note, and he didn't know where she was. He went next door to play.

When Mother got home, she was angry that Josh wasn't there. She called around the neighborhood and found him next door. She went over and asked him angrily why he had not left a note.

Josh yelled at his mother that he had gone home when he said he would and she was not there. Since she had not left a note, he didn't see why it was necessary for him to. Mother said that Josh was being disrespectful and that this was no time to argue! He began to kick his feet and scream. Mother dragged him out the door.

Josh felt that he had been treated unfairly because Mother expected him to leave a note when she had not done so herself.

Parents often expect children to obey rules that they themselves forget to follow.

Children will copy the behavior they see in the adults around them. If one parent is sloppy and leaves messes around, we should not be surprised if the children do likewise. If one parent curses, lies, smokes, drinks, screams, hits, or falls apart—then we should expect to find the same behavior in the child. If one parent is habitually late, why be surprised when the child follows his example?

If one parent does not like to go to church and frequently makes excuses, the child will surely want to stay home. If a parent exceeds the speed limit or sanctions minor infractions of the law (allows the child to drive before he is old enough to have a learner's permit), the child will feel that he likewise has the right to bend rules and assume they do not apply to him.

We cannot expect behavior of our children that we do not expect of ourselves. If we want them to obey laws, follow directions, or exhibit admirable traits, we have to make sure that they have an available model in us.

> Several adults and teenagers were spreading sand and raking the muddy ballfield, trying to make it playable for the afternoon Little League games. Brett was sitting on the bleachers watching them. After about fifteen minutes he called out, "Work Slaves." The father who was nearest the bleachers heard him.
>
> He stopped raking, turned to Brett, and said, "Instead of yelling, why don't you grab a rake, you lazy little punk, and help us work on the field?"

"Brett laughed and said, "I don't have to. My team isn't playing today."

"Well," said the father, "I hope it rains the next time your team is scheduled to play." He continued to rake a few minutes, and then stopped to ask Brett what team he was on. When he was given an answer, he retorted, "Your team must be in the baby league at the other field because you certainly don't act like a real ballplayer."

Receiving no reaction from Brett, he then threatened to report the boy's sassiness to his coach, and added, "I wouldn't be surprised if you aren't allowed to play ball for the league next year."

By this time, he was so upset that he laid his rake down and left the field. He mumbled, as he left, about ungrateful, punky kids who didn't appreciate what they have.

Brett left the field, mumbling also that he hated the man and was glad that he didn't have to play on a team with his son.

If Brett had been treated differently, he might have been persuaded to help the men instead of insulting them. There are many ways this father might have tried to win him over instead of reacting to him and alienating him further.

It was obvious that for some reason Brett had a bad attitude. Recognizing this, an adult could refuse to react negatively, and instead, could brush it off with, "Hey, we need some help. How about grabbing a rake." If this didn't work, he might say, honestly, "It bothers me for you to talk to us that way. If you would help us, we could finish sooner."

Or the man could have just ignored the remark and continued working. At least he would have been displaying mature behavior (not to allow himself to be drawn into a confrontation). Name-calling breeds resentment. By calling Brett "a lazy punk," he probably made him angrier and more determined not to help in any way.

Adults working with sports teams play a unique role in the lives of children and have an excellent opportunity to teach mature and sportsmanlike qualities to the many young men and women who look up to them.

Ross had his learner's permit and had been driving for two months. He had a date to go to the movies and asked his parents if he could take the car.

"No, you cannot, Son. You know you can't drive alone for two more months."

"But we're going to double date and Neil has his license. Can't I just drive alone to his house? I certainly won't get caught going two miles. You're such a stickler for rules."

"What do you think, Sonny?" Mom asked. "Do you think Ross would be safe going a couple of miles without a licensed driver in the car?"

"No, I don't think it's a good idea, Marsha. It would be just his luck to get caught, and then he would have his learner's permit revoked."

"Aw, c'mon, Dad. Everybody else does it. Brian's dad lets him and he's the coach. Brian never got caught."

"Well, it's up to your dad, Ross. Whatever he says goes."

"I say 'no,' then, and that's that!"

Ross went to his room and slammed the door behind him.

Ross's parents had an open discussion and made a good decision, but for the wrong reason. They decided on the basis of whether or not Ross would get caught, rather than the rightness or wrongness of his actions.

If we want our children to respect law and order, we have to show such respect ourselves and not permit them to bend rules, even if the chances are that there will be no consequences to suffer.

Children who are allowed to break minor laws when they are young usually generalize this behavior and feel justified in committing serious infractions as they grow older.

The first grade teacher had graded the children's worksheets and given smily faces to the ones whose papers were perfect.

When Martha received her worksheet, there was no smily face on it. Seeing that other children had received them, she began to cry. She put her head down on her desk and sobbed softly to herself.

At first the teacher didn't notice.

"Mrs. Dennis, look. Martha is crying," offered her little friend, Nancy.

Mrs. Dennis came over to the table. "What's wrong with you, Martha?" she asked in a sharp voice.

Martha didn't respond.

"I think she's crying because she didn't get a smily face on her paper," suggested Nancy.

"Martha, look up here. Is that why you're crying? Martha!" She lifted the child's head so that she could see her face.

"Answer me, Martha," Mrs. Dennis shook the child's arm.

Martha looked down, without saying a word.

"Now, look here. That's ridiculous—to cry when you don't do a good job on your paper. Suppose every child in here cried when she didn't get a smily face. We would have a bunch of crybabies. Now straighten up. I'm not going to let you leave until you stop crying. Your mother is probably outside now to pick you up. If you want to go home, you'd better stop crying. Do you hear?"

She dropped the child's arm and left her alone.

Martha put her head back down on the desk.

Mrs. Dennis began calling the children to line up to go home. She didn't call Martha. After the others had left, she came over and pulled her up.

"Come on. I'm going to have a talk with your mother."

They went together outside to find Martha's mother, who was waiting in the car.

"Mrs. Dyckman, I need to talk with you. Martha has been crying because she didn't get a smily face on her worksheet. Now, I am not going to tolerate her tears. She is much too old for that. I don't know why she thinks she has to be perfect all the time, but you will have to do something with her. I am simply not going to have a crybaby in my room."

Mother was upset and felt sorry for Martha. She opened the car door for her daughter as she responded to the teacher. "All right, Mrs. Dennis, I'll talk to Martha."

As they drove off, Martha put her head on her mother's lap and cried louder.

Most likely, Martha has at least one parent like her—a perfectionist—not satisfied unless he excels in everything he does. Whether consciously or unconsciously, these standards have been passed along to her. By age five, she has already internalized them. She is unhappy with herself when her work is not perfect. This is unfortunate and could have negative outcomes if the pressure is not lifted.

It is up to the adults in her life to lighten up on their expectations of her. Otherwise she will become fearful, anxious, and cautious—afraid to take risks for fear of disappointing those who expect her to be perfect.

Mean What You Say and Say What You Mean

Marijo is sitting at the dinner table eating with Mother and two guests. At frequent intervals, she loudly calls to Mother, "I don't like that!" about some food on her fork which she has not yet tasted. Jokingly Mother says, while touching the fork with her fingers, "Don't you dare eat that," in an exaggerated, sweet voice.

Marijo then eats the food, laughing.

This is repeated many times during the meal, usually when the adults are engaged in conversation.

The dinner is interrupted by Marijo's outbursts. She learns that her mother really wants her to DISOBEY and do the OPPOSITE of what she tells her to do.

The most important point in this case is the mixed message that Mother gave to Marijo. Children learn more from our non-verbal cues than from our words: Mother's words were, "Don't you dare eat this food," but her tone of voice was saying the opposite, "I want you to eat." The child was enjoying the playfulness and therefore obeying her non-verbal language.

Although Mother may think it's funny to trick Marijo into eating, she will not be amused later when she tells her daughter to "come here," and she runs the opposite way.

Marijo could easily adopt her mother's behavior and learn to mask the truth herself. Her mother won't like it then, when she asks who broke the glass and Marijo says, "Daddy did it."

If we want our children to be honest and obedient, we should be careful from the very beginning to say what we mean and mean what we say. We lose our credibility otherwise.

Young children are refreshingly open and honest. It is easy to tell when they are sad, happy, angry, or tired. We adults need to take a cue from them.

Unfortunately many of us fail to be honest with children about our feelings. We say one thing and mean another. This comes from our mistaken notion that we, as parents, are supposed to be paragons of virtue—always loving, kind, cheerful, and happy. When our feelings are negative, we have a tendency to feel guilty and try to deny them or cover them up. In reality, this causes problems, not only for ourselves, but also for the children in our charge.

For example: Brady comes home from school and finds Mother frantically scrubbing the kitchen floor. She appears upset. "What's wrong?" he asks, to which she forcefully snaps, "NOTHING." Her body language and tone of voice have given one message, while her words have given another. The child has received a "mixed message," which confuses him and forces him to come to his own conclusions about "what's up."

Because of their egocentricity, children have a tendency to blame themselves for trouble that they cannot identify. In the case above, Brady may withdraw from his mother, wondering what he had done wrong. He may conclude that

Mother has found the broken cup in the trash can, or that she was still angry because he had spilled juice at breakfast.

Mixed messages such as the one Mother had given Brady make children aware of our deceits and ultimately destroy their trust in us. They can eventually cause children to become unable to recognize and deal with reality.

Every child needs to know that he can believe what his parents say. It is unrealistic to think that we will never be angry, worried, discouraged, and tired. We build artificial relationships when we deny our human weaknesses and imperfections, which may cause our children to build walls around themselves and be afraid of closeness. We create a safer climate for our children when we can accept and own up to our negative feelings.

When our bodies, tone of voice, and words all speak the same language, children will grow up happier and more secure, not feeling that they must whitewash their mistakes and disguise their feelings. More importantly, they will then be free and able to form close and genuine relationships with the ones they choose to love as they mature and grow away from us.

At an outing to the city park, Jenny, seven, climbed up on the picnic table, stuck her hand into the pickle jar and took a big pickle. She stood on top of the table, waving her pickle and called to her mother, "Look, I got a pickle." Her mother told her to get down off the table and to put the pickle back. She added that Jenny was going to "turn into a pickle" if she ate another one. Then Mother shook her head, laughed, and resumed her conversation with other family members.

Jenny stayed on top of the table, ate that pickle and another one. Laughing back at her mother, she openly defied her and learned that Mother does not mean what she says.

Mother should have decided right away whether she was going to allow this behavior or not. If she decided that it was unacceptable, then she should have stated what she wanted Jenny to do (get off the table) and then followed through to see that she obeyed (moved to the table and helped her get down).

Mother's method of (not) handling the situation taught Jenny that Mom does not mean what she says: Jenny will not turn into a pickle and she does not have to get off the table when her mother tells her to. The next time Mother tells Jenny to stop a certain behavior, the chances are that she will not obey her.

Daddy had been asked to come to the school for a parent conference. Since he did not have a babysitter, he brought all three of his children with him. He told them to play on the playground while he talked with Adam's teacher.

The conference had just begun when Adam appeared at the door. Daddy said to him, "I told you to stay on the playground. What are you doing here?"

"I wanted to hear what you were saying about me," he replied in a whiny voice.

"Well, I guess that makes sense," Daddy said, "I don't think Mrs. Bauer will mind."

The teacher responded, "There are a few things I would like to discuss with you in private, and then Adam can join us."

The child sidled up to his father, whining and clinging, "No, I want to stay, Daddy."

"Come on, now. You behave yourself and I'll get you some ice cream on the way home."

Adam's two sisters appeared at the door. Daddy called to them, "Come on in and play with Adam in the corner while I talk with Mrs. Bauer. The children were delighted with the invitation, and they happily began playing with the toys. Soon they were throwing things and yelling to Daddy, "When are we going to get ice cream?"

Mrs. Bauer was agitated about this turn of events. She was irritated that the children were being given free rein in her room. She lost her enthusiasm for the conference and cut it short. She made a decision not to invite Adam's father in for more conferences. In the future, she would talk with him by phone.

As it turned out, the conference was a waste of time for both the teacher and the father. Adam learned that the way to receive attention and to get his way was to whine and disobey instructions. All three children learned that what Daddy *says* is not what he *means.*

The children had Daddy on the spot, and they knew it. Daddy lost face when he backed down and allowed Adam to stay when he had already asked him to remain on the playground. Then once he gave in for one child, he felt that he had to give in for all three.

Daddy should have tackled the problem as soon as it arose. When Adam arrived, he should have been firm. "Adam, I asked you to stay on the playground. Please go back there and wait for me." If he refused to leave, Daddy could have taken him by the hand and shown him to the door.

Daddy needed to take time to teach his children to obey him. He could have made his expectations clear before they left home. If necessary, he could have reminded them again at the school and made sure that they understood exactly what he expected. He could have promised them initially that if they played nicely on the playground while he talked with the teacher, then they could stop for ice cream on the way home. By promising this *after* they already disobeyed him they learned that they could get ice cream by ignoring their father's requests. We should be careful to make such arrangements and negotiations *before* children have had a chance to misbehave, and not after.

Parents who are at the mercy of their children do not gain their respect. Children need to know that the parent is in charge. With patience, firmness, and consistency, parents need to be willing to devote whatever time and energy it takes to back up their expectations with action.

Have Confidence in Your Decisions

Judd's parents had recently separated. Since they only lived a short distance from each other, they had decided that it would be best for him to spend two days with each parent and then switch. This would give him alternate weekends with each, and would give them equal amounts of freedom. The marriage counselor had suggested this arrangement, and they had agreed that it would be best for all concerned.

When they had confronted Judd, nine, with their decision to separate, he had been quite upset. He screamed and yelled, threw things, and told his parents that they were both stupid.

They had accepted his anger and allowed him to express himself freely.

When the time came to separate, he packed his things and left with his mother.

In two days, when it was time for him to ride the school bus to his dad's house, he returned instead to his mother's. When his father got home from work and did not find Judd, he called his wife.

His son answered. "Hey, Judd, why are you at Mom's? You were supposed to come here. You knew that. What happened?"

"I'm not coming there until next week. I decided that I wanted to spend every other week with each of you. That suits me better. So, I'll be there on Saturday."

"Did Mom tell you that would be okay?" Dad was angry.

"I didn't tell her yet. She's still at work."

"Well, I don't like it. That was not the plan. You know you were supposed to come here, and you should have followed through. I'm coming to get you—now."

"Oh, no, you aren't. I won't come with you. I'm staying here." Judd hung up the phone.

Dad was mad. It didn't suit him at all for Judd to change the plans. He waited for his wife to get home and called her. Their conversation was strained.

"Well, I don't see that it matters that much," she said. "I think you're making a mountain out of a molehill. Hasn't he gone through enough? Let him stay. I don't care. It's not worth the hassle." She hung up.

Dad was angry. He was uneasy that a nine-year-old had been allowed to reverse a decision that had been carefully made by three adults. He was afraid that Judd would keep on making decisions that were not his to make—and, in the long run, would feel that he did not have to obey any rules if they did not suit him.

Judd's father had a valid point. A nine-year-old cannot possibly know what is best for him in all situations. He needs the security of knowing that people who are older and wiser and who have his best interests at heart will step in to enforce rules if necessary.

Dad's hunches are well-grounded. Judd will gain strength in the fact that his counter plan worked, and this will give him the incentive to continue to "be the boss." In time, both parents may feel that no matter what they tell him to do, he will only obey if it suits him.

This is not to say that Judd's feelings and opinions should not be considered. Dad could have said, "Your mother and I will talk with the counselor about this at our next session, but for now, the present plan sticks. I'm coming to get you."

At a time of disruption, such as divorce, parents are more vulnerable and shaky. This often causes them to doubt their own judgment and to be easily persuaded to back down.

Especially at such times of uncertainty and disruption, however, children need a life they can count on as well as parents who are still able to stick with wise decisions on their behalf. In the long run, the child will emerge more secure and stable—and able to accept decisions over which he has no control.

Jill had just begun nursery school. She was very excited and eagerly got herself ready to go. One morning, she complained that she had a stomach ache and wanted to stay home. Her mother let her, but as soon as the car pool had gone by, the stomach ache mysteriously disappeared.

The next morning, Jill dawdled.

"Hurry up," her mother coaxed, "or you'll miss the carpool."

"I don't want to go to school. My foot hurts. I think it's broken."

"What? Let's see your foot." Mother took a look and saw nothing wrong. The child had been walking fine, until she suddenly realized that her foot was giving her problems. Then she had developed a limp.

"Oh, come on now," Daddy said, as he came into the room. "There's nothing wrong with your foot. One day at home and you want another one. Nothing doing. Get ready, young lady, this minute!"

"Oh, Fred," Mother pleaded. "Let's not make her go. What if her foot is really hurt? I would be embarrassed if her teacher called me from school. I'm going to be here today anyway. It's all right if she stays home."

"You're spoiling her, Suzanne," Daddy told his wife. "You're going to be sorry."

For the next two mornings, Jill cried and Mother and Daddy argued about how to handle it. Mother thought they should take her at her word, but Daddy felt that she was manipulating them.

It would be wise for this mother and father to decide between them whether or not they thought nursery school was a good idea for Jill. They should not allow her to dictate to them. They might talk it over with the teacher, or observe the class to be sure that the placement seemed right for their child.

Then, if they decided that she should go, they should tell her their decision. "You are going to nursery school. You may go crying, or you may go happily. It is up to you. But you will go."

When children feel that their parents mean business, they are usually more willing to comply with their wishes.

Parents Need to Get Their Own Act Together

Mother was washing dishes and Daddy was sitting at the kitchen table reading the newspaper. Tom, three, got a toothpick and began to stick it in his gum. Mother asked him to give her the toothpick. He refused. Mother took the toothpick from him, and he flung himself on the floor nearby and started to kick at Mother. She tried to ignore him and attend to her dishes.

Daddy saw Tom kicking at Mother and picked him up, turned him across his knee and spanked him.

Mother was upset at Daddy for intervening and for spanking Tom. They got into a heated argument about child-rearing in general, and spanking in particular. Mother told Daddy that he should stay out of it when she is handling a situation, and he yelled back that she is too easy on Tom and shouldn't let him get by with kicking her. For a half hour, they argued loudly.

Meanwhile Tom wandered away into the den, where he began to tear up a magazine.

This is a common scene in many households: child causes problem—parents disagree over method of handling—parents get into argument—child becomes more upset—problem is not solved—a larger problem is created.

Although no two people agree on every issue concerning child-raising, the more they can settle *before* problems occur, the more effective their discipline will be.

It is not unusual for parents to disagree over child-raising techniques. In fact, it is good for children to learn that there are different adult points of view. This is healthy. They also need to see that adults can settle their differences, solve their problems, and still love each other even when they disagree.

Children have a tendency to blame themselves for family trouble. Dr. Rudolph Dreikurs, author of *Children, the Challenge,* says that a misbehaving child is a discouraged child. In the case mentioned above, Tom was probably feeling very discouraged when he went into the den and started tearing up a magazine. He had caused a problem between his parents and they ended up having a terrible argument.

Lori was playing in the living room when her mother called to her.

"Lori, it's time to pick up your toys now," she said. "We're almost ready to leave for church." Since Lori didn't answer, Mother repeated herself several times. Finally, Father stepped in and told Lori to pick up her toys immediately.

When Lori didn't respond, Father walked over and said, "Lori, did you hear me? Do I have to spank you to get you to listen?" He then picked Lori up, put her across his knee and spanked her bottom. Lori ran to her mother crying.

"Here, Lori," she said, "I'll help you pick up the toys." She squatted down and cleaned up the entire mess.

Father was fuming. "Now why did you do that, Noreen?" he said to his wife. "What do you expect Lori to learn from that? Honestly, no wonder she never listens to either of us. She knows you'll step in to save her."

"Come on, it will be all right. Daddy's not mad at you." Mother comforted Lori as they left. In the car, she held her child on her lap.

Lori's parents did not speak to each other all the way to church. Lori snuggled up to her mother and sucked her thumb.

When parents disagree over child-rearing techniques, children are confused and end up playing one parent against the other. This frequently causes hard feelings, and although the child seemingly wins the short-term battle, in the long run she loses all the way around.

Children need to feel that parents know what is best. When they cause their parents to argue, they develop an exaggerated sense of their own importance and have more control than they can handle. This leaves them insecure and uneasy.

If parents disagree over child-rearing techniques, it is best to discuss the disagreements when the child is not present. (For the most part, it is wise for parents to support one another in the presence of the child.) Later, it is fine for a parent to admit to his child that his judgment was hasty, and, having had a chance to think it through, he has reconsidered.

In this case it would have been better for Father to leave the room and let Mother handle the situation. If he did step in, Mother should have let him handle the problem. In this case, the actions of each made the actions of the other ineffectual.

Mother and Daddy had taken Jimmy, eleven, shopping to buy him a birthday present. When they got in the store, Daddy began to make suggestions.

"How about a calculator or a microscope? You could use either one to help you at school. What do you think of a chess set? I used to love to play chess."

Jimmy showed little interest in the items Dad mentioned. Instead, he started looking at the Star Wars Activities Packages and race car sets.

"Those are a waste of time, son. I'm not going to spend my money on things like that. You need something to stimulate your brain. Those are baby toys."

"Now, Ed, it is Jimmy's birthday, not yours. Let him choose whatever he wants," Mother intervened.

"You spoil him to death. That's what's wrong with him now. You're afraid to say 'no.' Well, I'm putting my foot down. Either a calculator, a microscope, or a chess game."

Jimmy came up to his parents, holding the race car set he had chosen.

"I'm sorry, Jimmy, but your father says that you must choose between a calculator, microscope, or chess set. I don't agree with him. I know it's *your* birthday, but he thinks *he* should decide what you want." Mother said sarcastically. "So make up your mind."

"I don't want any of those," Jimmy started crying. "I want this." He threw the race set on the floor. "If I can't have it, I don't want anything. That's not fair. It's *my* birthday."

Well, see what a mess you made," Mother said to her husband. "Since you made it, you solve it."

Embarrassed by the scene Jimmy created, Dad walked out of the store.

Mother begged her son to stop crying. "C'mon, Jimmy. Pick up the race car set. We'll get it. It's your birthday. Daddy had no right to tell you what you could or couldn't get."

Jimmy stopped crying immediately. He picked up the toy and handed it to his mother. She quickly purchased it and together they left the store to find Daddy.

All the way home, Daddy said nothing to either his wife or son. Once there, he went straight to bed.

Too many scenes like the one cited above can quickly put a strain on a marriage.

Obviously Dad is accustomed to losing such battles and Jimmy is used to winning them. Mother has assumed the role of the negotiator and the decision-maker. This is not atypical. Jimmy will probably become more demanding and manipulative if his parents don't make an effort to get their own act together and present a united front to their son.

Mother had fixed her husband's favorite breakfast—french toast—and called him to eat. When he came into the kitchen, he said that he didn't have time for breakfast, his stomach hurt anyway, and he would be late to work if he stopped to eat. Putting on his coat, he reminded his wife to get the car inspected and not to forget to pick up his suit at the cleaners.

"You'd better take the car early, because you remember what happened the last time. You spent the day with Fae, and by the time you got to the station, it was too late."

Without saying anything else, he left through the kitchen door.

Mother was upset. She felt let down. She had gotten up early enough to fix a nice breakfast and expected to receive some gratitude and attention from her husband. Instead, he gave her orders and reprimanded her for previous mistakes.

She felt like crying, but instead, went to the steps and called the children.

"Paul, Catherine, hurry up. Your breakfast is getting cold. I'm tired of being a slave around here. C'mon or I'll throw your breakfast away too."

Catherine came down the steps, slowly. "What's wrong, Mom? Did you get up on the wrong side of the bed? I came as soon as you called me. Where's Dad?"

"He couldn't take time to eat. You know. Work! Work! Work! He can just get his own breakfast from now on. I'm not going to waste my time."

"Paul, what's wrong with you this morning?" Mother called again. "Shake a leg. Don't ask me to take you to school if you miss the bus."

Finally, when Paul came down, he was grumbling because he couldn't find one of his shoes.

"I know I left it under my bed. Did you clean my room? Did you put it somewhere?"

"Oh, sure, Paul, I needed a shoe and wore yours. Sorry about that!" Mother replied sarcastically.

Grumpy and irritated with his mother, Paul carelessly bumped against the table, spilling his sister's juice.

"Now look what you've done, clumsy. Won't you ever grow up? I don't know how I got so lucky. Just get out of here. I can't take any more. Get out!"

Paul and Catherine both cleared out of the kitchen, leaving Mother with spilled juice and half-eaten french toast.

Later in the morning, when Paul's teacher gave a pop quiz, he decided not to try. He balled up his paper and threw it away.

Parents need to realize that the atmosphere in the home often sets the stage for the rest of the day. Like the stone causing a chain of ripples in the water, the attitudes and actions of the parents can affect those they love for many hours to come.

It takes effort to behave in positive ways toward family members. It is easy to take them for granted and to become careless. When family members—especially the parents—are warm, polite, and supportive of each other, the children have a strong foundation from which to start the day. When disappointments and challenges come, they have the resistance and strength they need to face them.

Mother and Daddy had been arguing about whether or not they could afford to buy a car. Mother didn't think they should spend the money and Daddy disagreed. The argument got hot and heavy and gradually other issues were mentioned.

"We would have more money if you would plan ahead what you spend. I don't see why you can't make a budget and stick with it. You are impulsive and don't plan ahead. Whatever you want you get, without thinking whether or not we can afford it." Daddy got louder and louder.

Mother's feelings were hurt, so she flared back.

"Now it's all my fault. I can't help inflation. Everything costs more. Why don't you try buying the food and clothes and paying the bills for a change? You'd see how hard it is. I'm tired of getting the blame. It's not fair."

Mother jerked the hair dryer she was using out of the wall socket and threw it on the floor. As she ran out of the room, Dad slammed the door behind her.

Downstairs, Stephen, fourteen, and Nancy, twelve, were listening. When they saw Mom running down the stairs, they knew she was angry.

"What's wrong?" Nancy asked Mom as she came running down the stairs.

"Nothing. Nothing. I just get blamed for everything. I'm sick of it all.

I'm leaving. He can just pay the bills and run the house and see how he likes it." She went out the front door, slamming it behind her.

Nancy started after her mother.

"Leave her alone," Stephen said as he grabbed his sister. "She'll be back."

"Let me go! Get your hands off me." Nancy slapped Stephen across the face.

Stephen grabbed her hands and wouldn't let go. She screamed and kicked.

Daddy came downstairs, furious with both of them.

"Go to your rooms. You know that fighting is not allowed in this house." He pulled Stephen off Nancy and slapped him hard.

Instead of going to his room, Stephen walked out the back door.

"Come back here, young man," Dad called.

Stephen kept walking, then started running down the street.

What started out to be a disagreement between Mother and Dad spread to the children—until all four of them were involved.

Parents teach their children every day. They are modeling coping strategies by the way they handle stress and deal with disagreements and problems. In this case study, the parents yelled, threw things, slammed doors, and walked away from their problems. The children are already imitating their modes of behavior.

Disagreements are inevitable. We would not want to raise children in an environment where people always agreed or where one parent made all the decisions.

It is good for children to know that parents do not always think alike. It is important for them to grow up knowing that there is no one adult point of view. However, they need to learn the art of rationally solving problems by discussion and compromise.

Children are lucky if they have parents who model the skills needed to handle stress in ways that are productive. Then they will learn the beauty of reconciliation and the happiness that comes from working out differences and restoring relationships.

Questions and Answers

Q. *Is it our imagination, or does our baby really "act up" when my husband and I argue? It seems to us that when we are upset, he cries more, sleeps less, and is generally more fussy. Is that possible?*

A. It is not unusual for children to sense their parents' upsets and to "act up" in one way or another. It is important that we learn early to work out our differences as quickly and maturely as possible. Then our children will learn that, even though we have differences, we can cope with them and still love each other and live together in peace and harmony.

Q. *How do parents counteract the undesirable traits that children pick up from their peers? Our daughter, two-and-a-half, is starting to come into contact with a child who exhibits undesirable behavior (name calling, bad language, and dirty words). How should I handle this? Am I drawing attention to this behavior by sending him home when these things happen, or should I wait for my daughter to pick up his manners and then explain to her that it is not acceptable? We try to avoid this child as much as possible, but this is becoming hard to do.*

A. Sooner or later children will be exposed to bad influences. A two-and-a-half-year-old child is still trying very hard to follow her parents' lead, and although she can and will imitate the behavior of other children, her parents' reactions to her behavior will determine the extent to which it is maintained.

If we can be casual and unimpressed by naughty words, if we are careful not to make a big deal of them, and if we expose our children to other children whose behavior is more desirable, chances are that any little bad habits that they pick up will soon diminish in importance, for them as well as for us.

Q. *My husband and I have a big disagreement about taking our five-year-old son to church.*

Last Sunday, we suggested that he stay in the nursery, but he insisted that he wanted to go to church. We gave in reluctantly. However, when we got in the service, he changed his mind and said he wanted to go home. My husband felt that we should make him stay, but I couldn't stand it. I took him by the hand and left. My husband was angry with me all the way home. What do you think?

A. I agree with your husband. You should have agreed ahead of time about the conditions of the bargain. Your son should have understood that if he chose to go to church, it meant that he was making an agreement to behave during the entire service.

By allowing him to change your plans, I think you are giving him too much control and making decisions for you that you should be making yourself.

Next time I would leave him in the nursery and explain that he lost the privilege of making the choice for awhile. Later, you will let him make the decision again, when you feel that he understands the terms of the bargain.

Q. *My husband and I have a running argument we would like for you to settle. Our twelve-year-old son is small for his age, and when we go to parks and movies, my husband says that Bobby is eleven.*

I feel this is wrong. Even though we save money, I'm afraid that in the long run Bobby will learn that it is all right to lie. What do you think?

A. I'm on your side. Children learn more from our actions than our words.

Q. *My husband and I disagree over many child-rearing issues. I have read books, attended lectures, and taken classes on parenting, and I feel that my views are more modern and effective. We have big arguments in front of the children. I know they are tired of listening to it. He is very strict and hard on the children. I can see that they are beginning to stay away from him. He won't listen to me or try any new methods. What can I do?*

A. This is a common problem.

The same techniques that we use with children to change their behavior works with spouses. We can learn to ignore the undesirable behavior—walk away from the situation—when our spouse is doing something we disapprove of. Be careful NOT to argue, beg, holler, preach, nag, embarrass, belittle, threaten, or reverse his orders. Silence is magic.

Then when your spouse is doing something you like, be sure to praise, thank, brag on, talk to, and give your attention to him.

Sometimes "recently converted" people make themselves so obnoxious that others would not give in or agree even if they wanted to. The best way to teach is by example. If we are patient, the other partner will see that your way is effective and getting results, and you will begin to notice some small changes in the right direction.

Q. *My trouble is with my in-laws. They are so good to us and love our children dearly, but they constantly give in to them. Our children can wrap their grandparents around their little fingers. If we tell them they can't have something, they can almost always get it from their grandparents. I'm beginning to resent them a great deal. I feel that our children are learning to beg and cry for what they want, and their grandparents fall for it. We have asked them not to give in, but they won't listen.*

A. This is not an uncommon problem. Many grandparents seem to differ from their children on child-rearing practices. The only suggestion I have is what you have already done, and that is talk with them about it. Tell them that you are afraid that your children will take advantage of their benevolence and also will develop the habit of begging and crying for what they want. Of course, your children have probably already learned to discriminate and to know when and where they can and cannot beg, plead, badger, and whine.

Therefore, since you have warned the grandparents, I would let this be their problem. If they continue to give in to the children, I would try to accept them for all their good qualities and be thankful that your children have grandparents who are alive and who care deeply for them.

Suggestions for the Week

Open up dialogue with friends, spouse, or family concerning the following:

Parents should Not:

1. Put their child's needs above all others.

2. Take sides raising the children or try to be the "favorite parent."

3. Make their children's problems their own by attempting to solve them instead of letting the children find their own solutions.

4. Blame their mate for the child's weaknesses.

5. Take over the job of "child-raising" singlehandedly. Convince the mate that he/she is inept and in the way.

6. Convey to the spouse, verbally or non-verbally, that the child is the first concern and the marriage relationship is secondary in importance.

7. Belittle and undermine the mate in front of the child. Discount what he/she thinks and says and reverse his/her decisions.

8. Make "child-talk" the center of every conversation.

Parents Should:

1. Accept the fact that you will disagree over child-rearing techniques.

2. Conclude that one person cannot be both mother and father. Decide to be the best parent you can, and allow your spouse to be the best parent he/she can be. You are not responsible for his/her parenthood.

3. Talk as freely and as often as possible about methods of child-raising—especially when there is *no* problem.

4. Keep an open mind and be willing to try new techniques.

5. When a problem occurs between one parent and a child, let the parent involved handle the situation. Don't intervene, sympathize, or in any way undermine or alter what the other parent is doing.

6. If you disagree, wait until later, when you have a chance to discuss it in private, to talk about it.

7. Be willing to admit you were wrong. Let the child know that after thinking about it and talking it over, you have changed your mind.

8. If possible, read some books, or better yet, attend some classes *together*—on child-management techniques. Discuss and try out some new ways of handling things.

This week try to be:

Big enough to say you're sorry when you jump to conclusions or blame someone else when the fault is yours.

Brave enough to say "No" when it would be easier to say "Yes"—especially when you know that your "No" will make you unpopular and your child angry.

Courageous enough to take a good look in the mirror and honestly evaluate the self you see.

Strong enough to put forth the effort to become the person of your dreams.

Self-disciplined enough to work hard for the goals that you think are important.

Secure enough to look for and affirm the good you see in other people.

Patient enough to let your child learn from his own mistakes.

Loving enough to let him suffer the consequences of his actions.

Honest enough to tell the truth when your child comes to you with a question.

Sensitive enough to "be there" when he needs you.

Relaxed enough to realize the importance of spending time alone with your child each day.

Intelligent enough to realize that he has much to teach you if you will only listen.

Calm enough to stop in the midst of deadlines and rush hours to watch the sunrise, listen to the ocean, smell the spring rain, and feel the softness of sand beneath your feet—teaching your child to experience the beauty of God's earth.

Accepting enough to realize that your child is a separate person—with needs, qualities, strengths, and weaknesses unlike yours and unique to him.

Capable enough to cope with daily obstacles—to attempt to solve problems and not just complain about them.

Thoughtful enough to show respect to your own parents and other older people by sacrificing your time and energies for them.

Smart enough to rest when your body is weary, exercise when it is stiff, eat when it is hungry, and stop when it is full.

Kind enough to be concerned about the needs of others.

... and **WISE** enough to remember that if you want your child to grow up to possess these noble traits, it will be necessary for him to see them first in you.

Chapter Ten

Enjoy Your Children

The last and most important principle for raising happy, well-adjusted, and mentally healthy children is to enjoy them. Laugh with them every day. Let them know without question that they are the source of your happiness, that they bring you pleasure, and make your life richer.

Remember how it feels to walk into a room full of strangers and catch the eye of a friend. There is a moment of recognition—when you see a smile cross his face—and you know it is because of you. It gives you a warm glow, a feeling of importance and contentment.

Our children need to know that they do that for us. When they first entered our lives, they brought us joy and pride. We should try to keep those feelings alive and let them know that we are still proud to be their parents. It is up to us to help them become persons who respect others and are worthy of respect themselves.

The baby derives his sense of self from the faces he sees, the attitudes he senses, the touching he experiences. Eventually what he will believe about himself is what we believe about him. If we see him as capable, lovable, interesting, and adequate, that is what he will become. The way he feels about himself forms the core of his personality, and, in large measure, determines the extent to which he will be able to make good use of his abilities and opportunities.

When a child lacks a solid sense of his own identity, his inner world is a maze, and instead of being able to put his energies to use in productive ways, they are wasted trying to unravel the confusion and mystery within.

We need to convince the child that he is special. When we believe it, so will he. Most people who have succeeded in life attribute their success in part, at least, to some person in their past who believed in them—a teacher, a grandparent, a caring friend, or a parent.

The most priceless legacy we can give our children is to help them *like* themselves. After I conducted a workshop recently, a woman shared a beautiful story with me. When she was a little girl, she said, her face had been covered with freckles. It was apparent to her that her mother disliked them, for when she washed her face she would say, "Let's see if we can scrub those freckles off." Therefore, as a child, she was ashamed of her freckles. When she was fifteen, a man meeting her for the first time took a long look at her face, then said lovingly, "Oh, you are so lucky. A woman without freckles is like a night without stars!" She said that statement changed her life. From that day on, she started feeling proud to have freckles. Now she has her own little girl—with freckles. Needless to say, she has tried from the very beginning to help her child feel that her freckles make her very special.

When children possess the quiet contentment that says, "I'm glad I'm me," they have the strength to cope with stress, the ability to love, and the courage to become responsible, productive, and contributing members of society.

Children need space and freedom to become what they were created to become—not what we might choose for them to be. We must remember that we cannot make a rose out of a carnation.

We need to help a child find his strengths, his aptitudes, and the things he enjoys, and then capitalize on them. If he likes music, let him try it. If he likes to work with his hands, or be involved in sports, or loves animals, provide him with appropriate information and exposure. Give him opportunities to investigate and explore, and encourage him to take risks and give life his "best shot." Teach a child to believe in himself, and you've given him the best gift you can give. You've made the best investment you can make in his future.

Remember that our children are unique creatures. They have much to teach us —if we are open and free to learn from them. They bring to life a freshness, curiosity, and enthusiasm that we would do well to emulate.

As the gardener takes his cues from the plant, so the wise parent takes his cue from the child. If the growth is in the right direction, if the child is more mature, self-sufficient, and confident than he was a year ago, he should be encouraged to continue in the same direction. If there seems to be trouble—regression or stunted growth—we need to look for the source of the problem and maybe ask for help.

When a plant with strong roots meets an obstacle, it re-routes itself. When children who feel good about themselves have doors slammed in their faces, they face the problems head-on and look for alternatives rather than retreat or give up.

It is the job of the parent to provide the child with those strong roots.

> After Mike, eighteen, had left for school, Mother noticed that he had left globs of toothpaste in the sink. Irritated, she washed them out, thinking to herself, "Won't that boy ever learn? Who does he think will clean up for him next year, when he's away at school? I feel sorry for his roommate." She resolved to remind him to clean out the sink in the future.
>
> As she was walking down the stairs, she thought to herself, "Next year ...he won't be here next year—or probably ever again—to live here with us on a permanent basis. I'm really going to miss him. He's such a fine boy. I'm so proud of him. How could he be old enough to leave home? Where did those years go?"
>
> She rethought her decision to remind him about cleaning the sink. "That toothpaste isn't a big deal. I don't think I'll even mention it. After all, I'm going to miss seeing that toothpaste next year. I'll think of Mike every time I look at the clean sink in the bathroom." She stopped short, as she felt tears come to her eyes.

The years of parenting do fly by. It is important that we let our children be imperfect—just as we should allow ourselves to be imperfect.

Many battles aren't worth winning. Parents should not waste their time and energy dealing with the unimportant issues, for deep down they need to keep their eye on the goal: to prepare their children to fly away—equipped to manage their own lives, involved with but not dependent on others, actively engaged in pursuits that are both meaningful and productive, and able to freely give and receive love.

Wise parents will remember the old saying that there are only two lasting gifts we can really give our children: "one is roots, the other wings."

> One of the hardest days of my life was the day I watched our two oldest children drive off together early on a Saturday morning in September. They were on their way to college.
>
> I think I had dreaded that day for eighteen years, remembering in the back of my mind that we raise them to give them away, that we work hard so they can live without us, that, in the words of Kahlil Gibran, "though they are with us, they belong not to us," that we are "the bows from which our children as living arrows are sent forth."
>
> This had been a beautiful summer, full of "last" things: the last time we would go to the beach, charcoal-broil steaks, and go to the ice cream store together. My children laughed—even at the "last" breakfast, which no one was hungry enough to eat.
>
> I had spent the summer getting myself ready, and stayed awake most of the night hoping I could prolong daybreak. But the day was here and the car was packed—complete with her tear-stained Raggedy Ann and his favorite posters, pillow, and beanbag chair. Even our Irish setter sensed the impending separation as he slipped out the back door and nosed his way into the front seat of the packed car, hoping not to be left behind.
>
> There was nothing more to do, there were no more errands to run, or last minute things to buy. This "good-bye" was different from any in the past. It was good-bye to a whole era, the last chapter of the book. No more "What time shall I expect you home? Have you checked the mail? Do you need anything at the store? Are you all right? Wait 'till you hear this! Mama, where are you?"

It was over quickly. We all cried—a little more—as we hugged one last time. They were excited and happy, soon driving down the street and waving from the corner. A final, familiar toot and they were gone.

As I watched them go, I wondered how the years could have passed so quickly. It seemed only yesterday when I had peeked through that first-grade window with tears in my eyes to see her eagerly raising her hand to answer the teacher's question. Wasn't it just a little while ago that I had smiled to myself when he made a "patrol badge" in the first grade and wore it to school to impress his classmates?

It was time for me to move on. All my "lasts" had prepared me for the next chapter: a new era, different, with more time to devote to the child who was left, to my husband, our jobs, friends, and ourselves. More tears would be in vain, shed only by me, for me. I had shed enough and was ready to move ahead.

I walked slowly back into the house, upstairs to their "too-straight" rooms, to find a note left on the bed addressed to "Mom and Dad." I had one last cry as I read, "Thanks for believing in us and teaching us how to live and how to love. We will always be grateful for our 'roots.' P.S. This is probably the last note you will receive from us on this Saturday in September."

"Your children are not yours but only given into your care for a short while." —*Tracy Johnson*

"For life goes not backward nor tarries with yesterday."—Kahlil Gibran

How can I be sad? We are better off today than we were twenty years ago. Then we had no children, yet we were happy. Today we have reaped the rewards of parenthood. We have benefited in every way because we were forced to mature with our children, for our children, and through our children. We are the ones who should be grateful.

Our lives are richer, fuller, happier, more complete—because of the years we had you on loan. Thanks for all you taught us and the ways you helped us grow. Although I hope you learned a great deal from us, I am confident that we learned more from you. Godspeed.

Index

E

Eating problems, 81

Embarrassment, 16, 18-20, 25, 27, 118, 138, 171

Encouragement, 25, 167

Enjoyment of children, 227-232

Expectations, 25-26, 47-53, 56, 127, 138, 142, 203-205
 parental, 215

F

Fairness, 21-22, 75

Family rap sessions, 58, 141

Fears, 177-183, 193-194

Feelings, 22, 171-198

Firmness, 53, 72-75, 208-212

Friends, undesirable, 123, 131

Fussing, 52-55, 64, 108

G

Generalizing, 162

Gibran, Kahlil, 230

Gordon, Thomas, 191

Grades, 101

Grandparents, 222

H

Homework, 125-127, 130, 132

Honesty, 121, 188-193, 195, 206-207, 221

I

"I messages," 191-193

Illness, 152

Incentives, 85-87, 90-103

Independence, 106-107, 123

Individuality, 161

J

Jealousy, 150-153, 165

Johnson, Tracey, 232

L

Labeling, 23-26

Laughter, 227

Leaving home, 11, 123-124, 230-232

Lying, 221

M

Mealtime, 30, 81-82, 205

Misbehavior, 56, 61-64, 83, 118, 213, 220

Modeling, 132, 148, 199-225

N

Nagging, 52-55

Name-calling, 202

Negotiations, 53

New baby, 9, 150-152

Free!

Send for your complimentary issue of THE PARENT TRICKS OF THE TRADE NEWSLETTER, a newsletter full of imaginative, child-tested hints on every aspect of child-rearing.

☐ YES! Please send me a complimentary issue of
   THE PARENT TRICKS OF THE TRADE NEWSLETTER.

☐ YES! Please send me your FREE catalog of other
   fine parenting books, with titles like THE FATHER
   BOOK, MOTHERHOOD: YOUR FIRST 12 MONTHS,
   THE PARENTS WITH CAREERS WORKBOOK, and
   many others.

NAME_____

ADDRESS_____

CITY_____STATE_____ZIP_____

MAIL TO:

Georgia Norris

Acropolis Books Ltd.

2400 17th St., N.W.

Washington, D.C. 20009